What It Takes to Shatter Glass

WHAT IT TAKES TO SHATTER GLASS

EMBRACE YOUR POWER
AND CREATE THE FUTURE YOU WANT IN YOUR CAREER, LIFE AND RELATIONSHIPS

JESSICA GENDRON

NEW YORK
LONDON • NASHVILLE • MELBOURNE • VANCOUVER

What It Takes to Shatter Glass

Embrace Your Power and Create the Future You Want in Your Career, Life and Relationships

Published in New York, New York, by Morgan James Publishing. Morgan James is a trademark of Morgan James, LLC. www.MorganJamesPublishing.com

Proudly distributed by Publishers Group West®

ISBN 9781636982885 paperback
ISBN 9781636982892 ebook
Library of Congress Control Number: 2023943730

Cover Design by:
Jessica Gendron

Interior Design by:
Chris Treccani
www.3dogcreative.net

Dedication Page

With great hope for the future of women everywhere.
Until there isn't any glass.

Contents

Acknowledgments

To Jenni Robbins. Coach, agent, consultant, friend, colleague. There might be one hundred ways to describe who you are to me, but none of them feel like enough to truly encapsulate my gratitude to you for this book. You believed in me when I didn't quite believe in myself, when I was mired down in self-doubt. Without you this book would still be an idea in my head with nowhere to go. Thank you will never be enough.

To Sarah Rexford, my editor. Thank you for saying yes to this book and for all the patience you showed me as we worked through the editing process. You have immense talent. I marvel at how much smarter you made me sound. The book is better because of you. I am eternally grateful.

Dora Lutz and Rachel Rizzuto for your wise feedback and insight before the book was even edited. Your honest, constructive, and kind words helped to make this book better.

To the men. My allies, supporters, advisers, and past bosses who shaped the professional I am today, taught me important lessons, and shoved me out of my own way. To Bob, thank you for seeing the best in me and for opening my eyes to possibility. You altered the course of my life and have remained a colleague, supporter, and friend. You will always be family. To Jeremiah and Steve, thank you for believing in me when I was young, inexperienced, and naïve. You leaned in and made me a better professional, leader, and person when it would have been easy to lean out. Thank you for supporting me through all my weird career changes and challenging me to see things differently every time. To Josh and Matt for taking a chance on a girl, time and time again, and for letting me build a dream alongside you. I'm grateful for all the lessons I learned about business and myself along the way. To Dick for your wise advice, emphatic persistence to talk about the stuff that really matters and trusting me with the legacy of your business. You've shown me what true allyship looks like and our connection is more than professional, it's familial.

To the women who were bold enough to share their stories with me publicly. Thank you, Amber Fields, Amy Brown, Anette Landeros, Angela B. Freeman, Ann Marie Klotz, Anna Golladay, Anne Hathaway, Carolyn Mosby, Cindy Stellhorn, Erin Windler, Jamie Jones Miller, KJ McNamara (again), Marla Holdread, Mary Beth Oakes, Sarah Williams, Shari Rossow, and Stephanie Ewing. Your stories inspired me and helped to solidify my belief that self-advocacy is the most important skill we can master.

To my best girlfriends, Lauren, KJ, Ronnie, Meghan, and Alix. I thought of you and all our children as I wrote this book. My life would be incomplete without our powerful female friendships. One day I still plan to live in a lady commune with you.

To my girl posse, the band of women who support me, love me, and encourage me even when I don't believe in myself. While there are too many of you to name, you give me courage and determination when I have none. Your belief in me and what I am doing drives me forward.

To my parents and family. You are entwined into who I am. You shaped me into the fierce, determined, and passionate person

I am today. I am not who I am without you. Thank you specifically to my mom and dad, Carole and Tom. Mom, you pushed me to reach for the highest heights and to rely on myself. Dad, you taught me the value of hard work, how to solve problems creatively, and that everything in life is more enjoyable when we have a sense of humor about ourselves and the world.

Finally, to my husband, Ben, and our children, Emery and Oliver. For all the hours away writing, editing, reading, and studying that you supported me through. I could not have done any of this without all your love, grace and support. You are the reason I learned to advocate for myself. This is for you.

Preface

Chances are you picked up this book because you wanted to advance your career. You might feel stuck, burned out, or lost about what to do to get to the next level. Maybe you've recognized that you work too much, or you lack meaningful activities outside of your work and you want more balance. You may even be returning to the workforce after a hiatus or joining it for the first time. Whatever reason you picked up this book, thank you. Whatever you are feeling right now, I can assure you that you are not alone.

Throughout these pages, I will share my personal leadership journey, my theory on what it takes for women to succeed, and some anecdotes from other successful female leaders I have talked to. I'll give you some important cultural context that sheds light on why it is harder for women to succeed. Most importantly I will give you tangible and practical things you can do to overcome barriers and thrive in your life, relationships, and career.

This book is about advocating for yourself. It focuses on actionable ways you can develop your self-advocacy skills and get what you need and want from your career (and life). I believe that self-advocacy is what it takes to shatter glass ceilings. It is the single most important skill we must learn to overcome barriers, climb the ladder to success, and build the lives we want for ourselves. That's not fluff. I believe it and I know it's possible.

But why do I think that I possess the qualifications or expertise to write this book? Let me introduce myself.

I studied art in college at a mid-sized state university. I was the first in my family to go to college and it was the only college I could afford. I wanted to be a graphic designer. In my senior year of college, I, and another female classmate, were sexually harassed by a male art professor. When we reported the incident to the Dean of the college, he responded with, "There's nothing I can do. He's tenured."

This was the earliest moment in my life when I realized my gender mattered. From that point on, I decided not to pursue a career in graphic design. As an involved student leader, I turned to a trusted campus professional for advice about what to do next. He suggested a career in university administration. The next year, I started a Master of Science in Education program with dreams of one day being a university president.

My first job out of graduate school was at an elite private institution in administration. It was there I learned, again, that my gender mattered, and that the world was largely partial to white wealthy men. The politics and special favors were too much for me to bear. I left a year later to work for a small start-up. Over the next twelve years, I helped to grow and establish that start-up into a multimillion-dollar family of businesses. I spent my last five years as the CEO of all three of its companies.

During my time as CEO, my husband and I adopted two children from birth. The travel and stress of leading that company became too much. I left the company as our youngest was turning six months old and joined The Center for Leadership Excellence as their President. A year and a half later the COVID-19 pandemic hit and the owner offered the business to me to purchase (which I did).

Eight months later I was diagnosed with triple negative breast cancer. Over the next eighteen months, I completed eight rounds of chemotherapy, a bilateral mastectomy, twenty-five rounds of radiation, six months of oral chemotherapy, nine rounds of immunotherapy, and two additional surgeries—all while running a business, earning a Forty Under 40 recognition in Indianapolis, and parenting two young children in a global pandemic.

Today, I consult with global companies on creating more diverse, equitable, and inclusive workplaces including systems and culture. I am the trusted expert who helps executives understand the barriers that women and other underrepresented populations face every day at work (and in life) and what organizations can do to eliminate bias and create equity in their corporate practices. I work daily with women, whether speaking to aspiring college leaders, leading a class for emerging corporate professionals, or coaching C-level leaders. I hear their stories. I understand their challenges. I help them learn the skills necessary to overcome the barriers they face every day.

I tell you this so you'll turn the page and keep reading. I don't tell you this to stroke an overinflated ego. Frankly, I would have left this section out of the book entirely, but I kept getting feedback that I needed to share all that I had done and been through. I know what it's like. I've spent my career running up against most of the barriers women face in their careers and their lives.

What It Takes to Shatter Glass is my personal story laced with the experiences and stories of countless other women to whom I have talked. This book is not a fluff and sunshine, you go girl, feminist manifesto. I often lack the ability to sugar-coat. When I do, I have to intentionally craft those messages because that way of being is entirely unnatural for me.

This book is honest. It's straightforward. It's practical and it's actionable. If you want a feel-good feminist read that inspires you to go fight the patriarchy, this is not that book. There are a hundred more talented authors that can provide you with a you go girl memoir or an inspirational girl boss beach read. I'm much more pragmatic than that. I finish most of those books jacked up on inspiration but with a single question. "Okay, but now what do I *do*?" [1] This book is:

- A road map to help you take a stronger grip on your career
- Make moves faster toward your glass ceiling
- Accelerate your career growth
- Validate your experiences
- Give you tangible action steps to overcome what once felt insurmountable
- Create the life, relationships, and career to desire for yourself

This book is to help you be a valued voice at decision-making tables. This book is intended to help you shatter your own glass ceiling.

What you do is speak up for yourself. You self-advocate.

Among all the other noise and all the other business and leadership advice there is, I deeply believe that learning and leveraging the ability to advocate for ourselves, as women, is the single most important trait we can master.

Its impact reaches far beyond our careers into every corner and every relationship in our lives. It allows us to take control of our own realities, relationships, and futures. It's not easy and the journey is destined to have failure, but there is always success. One step more and one rung higher toward your glass ceiling *is* a success. So, grab your ladder. Let's shatter some glass.

Introduction

My first female role models were the confident, ball-busting, powerhouses of the '80s. They wore structured suit jackets and pencil skirts and walked into board rooms bossing everyone around. They scoffed at the women getting coffee and ate their male colleagues for lunch. They were honest, assertive, go-getters.

As a girl raised in the '80s and '90s, those were examples of what it meant to be a woman who shattered the glass ceiling. These women often gave up motherhood, relationships, and work-life balance all for the sake of climbing the corporate ladder. Once they achieved success, they protected their spot at the leadership table like the precious commodity that it was, often at the sacrifice of letting other women in. They were powerful, glamorous, and successful. I loved them. I wanted to *be them.*

My mother was a typist for an accounting firm from the age of eighteen until the day she retired. She worked at the same company for her entire career (albeit the name changed several times through mergers and acquisitions). She wasn't the woman in a power suit. She wasn't the one sitting at the leadership table making decisions with the guys. She was the one making copies and quite literally checking their work to make sure there weren't errors in their accounting.

As a young girl, I remember going to work with her on Saturdays during tax season. It was one of my favorite things to do with her. We would arrive at her office, a thirteen-story bank building that was one of the tallest buildings in our midwestern city center. We would walk into the marble lobby and pass the guard station on our way to the top floor. When the elevator door opened on the thirteenth floor, the scent of copy paper always wafted into the elevator car from the formal lobby.

Before heading to her desk, my mom would always take a loop past the partner offices to show me off, and we would always stop at the lone female partner's office, Helen, to say hello. Helen always seemed to be working harder than her male counterparts. She rarely looked up from her stack of papers to chat at length.

I always loved those laps around the office with my mom. The male partners were always so nice and chatty. I looked forward to seeing them. However, I'd always hope that when we passed Helen's office she wouldn't be there. She never seemed to have time to be bothered. It never occurred to me that Helen behaved that way because she was the only female partner in that firm. Her cold demeanor and inattentiveness were less about me and more about her trying to keep up, do more, and perpetually work to prove that she deserved her spot at the table.

I'm not sure my mother ever aspired to sit at a leadership table or climb the corporate ladder. I do know she wanted that for me. From the time I was young, she emphasized getting good grades, doing well in school, working hard, and going after whatever it was I wanted in life. She would push me and challenge me to succeed. She cheered me on from the sidelines. I didn't see a world with limitations and roadblocks at every turn. I saw a world of limitless possibility, even as a girl. It wasn't until much later that I realized how incredibly rare that was at the time.

I didn't realize how many roadblocks I would face, how isolating and alone, or how much work I would really have to do to ascend the corporate ladder. I thought everyone had to work as hard as I did to succeed. I lived in an illusion that it was just me, so I put my head down and worked. I didn't notice that there were a lot of people around me climbing the ladder faster than I was—and they didn't seem to be working as hard. I told myself that I was imagining it and that if I just worked a little harder, I would succeed, too.

It wasn't until I became a vice president and then a CEO that I realized my experiences climbing the ladder weren't unique. In fact, they were quite common. I discovered that many of the experiences that incited visceral anger and frustration in me were, in fact, quite similar to those of many other women. When I came to this realization, I was more frustrated and more angry than I was during my own leadership journey.

Why had no one told me this? Why was this a secret? Why was I, and seemingly most women, left to feel alone in these experiences?

College women are not taught how to successfully navigate the real world and ascend into leadership. They aren't told the truth about how hard it might be, the challenges they will face, the loneliness, the frustration, or the anger. No, in college, they pump women up with lies and romanticized notions about their futures.

There was a time when women in leadership roles were so rare that it was deeply competitive. It took some sort of magic to ascend into leadership as a woman. Merely being in the room, and not as the one fetching coffee, made you a unicorn of sorts. As a result, these women protected their seats at the leadership table like the scarce commodity it was. They didn't help other women succeed because another woman's success might mean their own demise. Women operated from a scarcity mentality during that time because there were so few women at the top.

As our world evolves, women in leadership are becoming less scarce. We see that women, when in leadership, often inherently create more space in leadership for others: other women, minorities, and underrepresented identities. As a result, the women's world has shifted to an abundance mentality. Instead of the mentality of, "There's not enough room at the table," the mindset has switched to, "There's plenty of room here, and if there isn't, we'll make more."

For the most part, the environment has shifted to where women in leadership are committed to their own success, but equally committed to leaving the door open behind them, helping others up the ladder, and inviting more voices to the table.

I live with that abundance mentality. As a result, I believe in equality *and* equity. I believe that more women in more leadership roles whether in business, politics, non-profits, etc., will make those organizations a better place. I don't just believe that women can make that kind of impact. I believe that a wealth of other underrepresented and marginalized identities can make that kind of impact, too. The more diverse a decision-making table is, the better the decisions are. I believe that with every fiber of my being.

But how do we, as women, ascend into leadership and find seats at decision-making tables? The truth is that it's not easy. You *can* be anything you want, but it's really *really* hard to get there. It's lonely. It's isolating. It's riddled with obstacles, detours, and landmines. It's not impossible, but it's not a stroll in the park either. The worst of it all is that no one teaches us how. We're left to figure it out on our own, which frankly, takes too long.

The McKinsey Institute publishes a report each year about women in corporate America called Women in the Workplace. It's common knowledge that women are underrepresented in leadership in corporate America. In fact, it's not just in top leadership positions, women are underrepresented at every level of leadership on the corporate ladder. We presume that there are fewer top leadership positions in companies, making the odds harder for women to land in executive roles. While this may be true, the problem begins much earlier. McKinsey found that the problem begins at the very first rung of that proverbial ladder [2].

While there are more women graduating from college each year than men, and women represent more of the entry-level workforce, they are promoted from entry-level into leadership less than their male peers. Based on the 2022 report, for every 100 men promoted from entry-level to manager, only eighty-seven women were promoted, and only eighty-two women of color were promoted [3].

This means that the problem isn't just about putting more women in executive leadership roles to even the ratio out or inviting a few token minorities to a meeting. We have to begin supporting women on their leadership ascension from their very first step into the workforce. That's a major shift in ideology for many companies. But why should a company invest in a new employee or a new leader when they're likely going to leave the organization in under five years? These organizations fail to see the potential return on investment. Instead, they invest their resources in a more sure bet, the mid-level and executive-track employees who are likely to stay longer and have some proven career success (positions that are predominantly held by men). That might be a decision that makes sense on the balance sheet, but it doesn't make sense for the long-term goal of gender equity in leadership, or for any kind of equality in leadership.

While females are a marginalized identity, I am cognizant that I identify as white. With my whiteness comes significant privilege. I recognize my whiteness and the power I am afforded as a result. I am deeply committed to using that power and privilege to make space for more women, particularly women who are different than me. I have been inspired by, learned from, and challenged by countless women from a diversity of backgrounds, experiences, and identities.

These women, their identities, and their experiences have made me a better person and leader. I know they have made every place they have touched better, too. We need more of that. More people embracing differences with a mindset of growth, understanding that difference is what has woven the fabric of America. A fabric is stronger the more fibers that are woven together. Thus, the same applies to leadership. Our leadership decisions and our leadership tables are stronger the more different, diverse, and disparate voices are at the table.

I am driven by one simple fact: more women in rooms where decisions are being made will make the world a better place.

Yet, I am dissatisfied with us merely being in the room. I won't rest until we are a valued and sought-after voice in decision-making. We know there are unique challenges that women face on their career journey and their ascensions into leadership. These challenges begin early in their career and have a compounding effect on their success.

Despite all these obstacles, I looked around and realized that I had made it. I had succeeded and there were lots of other women around me that had made it, too. I wanted to know *how.* What did it take for these women to succeed? How did they overcome these obstacles? What did they do to shatter glass ceilings and build the career of their dreams? What did they have to give up? I was desperate to know. I wanted to help other women succeed. I wanted the women after me to have a road map to circumvent, overcome, or bypass the challenges I, and other female leaders, had faced. I wanted to learn what women needed to do, no matter where they were on their ascension, to continue to climb the ladder. I wanted to give women the road map to shatter glass ceilings faster than I, and the women before me, did.

This is what has driven me to discover how women advance, succeed, and become that valued voice at decision-making tables. I wanted to know how the women who made it to those decision-making tables did it. I hoped to glean precious information from their stories so I could share it with every woman who has ever aspired to lead.

I set out on this crusade to crack the code. I wanted to interview successful female leaders about their experiences, what made them successful, who helped them along the way, and what advice they had for women on their journey to and through leadership.

So, I started asking regular, everyday, successful women. Not the unicorns of corporate America like Sarah Blakely (Spanx) [4] or Whitney Wolfe Herd (Bumble) [5], but everyday successful female leaders from all over the country and in a variety of industries: education, ministry, non-profits, Fortune 500 companies, lawyers, accountants, politicians. I wanted to know what it took for them to succeed. I wanted to capture their stories to inspire future female leaders. I wanted to learn their secrets so I could share them with as many women as I could. Unexpectedly, I found similarities in each of their stories and experiences. There were shared experiences that served as the road map to shatter glass [6].

Shattering glass and ascending into leadership is possible. I've seen it first-hand. The lynchpin is figuring out how we make it replicable. How do we create and give the roadmap to success to every woman who desires to ascend into leadership and shatter their own glass ceiling?

My hope is that this book will serve as that roadmap for women. So, cheers. May you read this and discover the path to shatter your own glass.

The Man-Hater Oath

I solemnly swear that hating men is not a requirement of being a feminist, reading this book, believing that women should have equal rights, opportunities, or equal seats in leadership and at decision-making tables. In fact, I solemnly swear that I will work to engage men in finding solutions, being better allies, and understanding how they benefit from systems in ways that women do not. I will begin by assuming no ill intent. I will understand that most men benefit from systems they had no hand in creating and are often unaware of how their behavior, leadership, decision-making, or ideology negatively impacts others.

Great. Glad we got that out of the way.

This book is for everyone. It's for people who want to learn how to overcome barriers in their careers and climb the leadership ladder. It's for individuals already in leadership who want to help others up the ladder. It's for men, particularly white men, who desire to understand how to be a better ally at work, to understand and use their privilege for good, and to help others have access to the same privileges and opportunities they were afforded.

This book is not fluff and sunshine. It's honest. It's not a feel-good "you go girl" manifesto. It's an actionable guide to navigate your leadership journey. Buckle up.

Part I:

Laying The Foundation

Chapter 1:
The Seven Competencies

When I started talking to successful female leaders, it was really nothing more than a pet project. At the start of the global coronavirus pandemic, everyone was searching for a way to make the lockdown productive. Some tended to their sourdough, while others learned to knit. I launched an interview series. In the series, I talked to female leaders about their leadership journeys, what contributed to their success, who helped them along the way, and what advice they would give to aspiring female leaders. I wanted to share their stories. I wanted to give women the microphone so we could learn from their experiences and be inspired by their voices.

It took no more than four interviews to start noticing common threads in the stories of these various women. The more I talked to these successful female leaders, the more I started to hear the similarities in how they talked about their successes. The stories were so similar. The advice they gave was aligned.

Sure, they would use different words or talk about things in their own context, but what they were saying was all the same.

I realized that what I had was so much more than just a series highlighting the journeys of female leaders. I had unknowingly stumbled on a road map. Had I just discovered the thing that women had been missing for so long? The thing that female leaders could never directly name, but had somehow organically discovered? Could I give aspiring female leaders the answers from the start so they could bypass all that time learning through their own experience? Could we leverage the wisdom of the women who came before them? I wanted to know, so I went back and coded the interviews to determine what the stories of female leaders had in common.

Through that process, I identified seven common themes:

- Self-Advocacy
- Self-Awareness
- Resilience
- Courage
- Intuition
- Relationships
- Communication

These themes, or competencies, were present in practically every interview with every woman I talked to. I was astounded. But were these competencies really the blueprint to shattering glass ceilings, climbing ladders, and achieving gender equality in leadership? I hoped so.

I began talking about these themes and working with aspiring female leaders to help them develop these competencies in themselves. The more work I did, the more I realized how critically underdeveloped these competencies were in women at various points in their careers. It became abundantly clear that women needed these competencies.

These were the skills that would help them accelerate their leadership journeys. I found that if women were stalled somewhere in their careers, it was often because they lacked development in one or several of these competencies.

I felt like I had found the Holy Grail.

It didn't feel real. I told myself over and over again that this wasn't a big deal. These findings were so seemingly natural to me. I couldn't quite believe that teaching women these skills would really do what I thought it might: jet-pack them up the career ladder.

Until it did.

Until every woman I spoke to and taught told me how helpful, practical, and insightful these skills were. I wasn't certain these findings could ultimately lead women to success until I watched women apply these new-found skills and succeed in ways that were inspiring.

It was then that I knew I had found my life's work.

Ever since I left what I thought would be my forever job in the middle of 2018, I had floated around directionless. I was searching for my purpose after I was left without one. I finally felt refocused. I had been given a gift, a gift that was intended to be given away.

What it Takes to Shatter Glass isn't a puff piece. I'll only use girly platitudes in jest. There's no, *girl power* or *#girlboss* mantras here. This book is only filled with strategies to overcome barriers, build necessary skills, rewrite our own socialization, and put more women at more tables where decisions are being made.

The Keystone Competency

I found that not all competencies are created equal. In fact, I found that there was one competency that mattered more than any other: Self-Advocacy.

While there weren't any female leaders that specifically said, "You need self-advocacy to succeed," nearly everything they shared pointed disproportionately to this competency in particular.

Over and over I heard female leaders talk about the concepts of self-advocacy. Further, they never discounted how important these concepts were. On the contrary, they emphasized them by how often the concepts appeared in our conversations.

I call this the Keystone Competency, not just because it was talked about the most by female leaders, but because it impacts every other competency. It serves as a critical component to making all the other competencies work. In fact, as you will find in this book, the other competencies support our ability to self-advocate.

Self-advocacy also happens to be the skill that women lack more than any other competency.

Self-Advocacy

From a young age, women are socialized to avoid bragging. We're taught that talking openly and bragging is an undesirable trait in women. Not only is it undesirable, but it's not to be trusted. It's selfish. In a culture where women are expected to be caretakers, concerning ourselves with the needs of others above our own, self-advocacy is a dirty little word. As a result, women become very good at advocating for the needs of others, often at the sacrifice of our own.

We will jump on a grenade for someone we love, happily march into a superior's office to demand a raise for a team member or vow to our best friend eternal hatred for a former partner without batting an eye. But stand up for ourselves? Rarely.

Men, on the other hand, lack these societal expectations. They're often expected to be the exact opposite: bold risk-takers who'll apply for jobs they're not qualified for or ask for raises they don't even know if they deserve. They're *expected* to make the first move. The result is that men speak up and ask for things most women couldn't even fathom asking for.

I discovered that of the female leaders I talked to, every single one of them spoke to self-advocacy. They learned to speak up for themselves in a variety of different places and different ways. As a result, they ascended the career ladder. Self-advocacy was by far the strongest theme of the seven competencies. Unfortunately, it is what I see women lacking the most throughout their leadership journey.

That's why this book is called *What it Takes to Shatter Glass*. Although there are seven competencies, self-advocacy is where we must start. What I have found is that in order to advocate for yourself successfully, to have to be good at communication and relationships. You have to have self-awareness. You have to have courage and intuition and resilience.

It's almost like self-advocacy is the umbrella under which all the other competencies sit. While each individual competency can exist separately from another, self-advocacy cannot. It does not exist without the others and becomes more powerful the more the others are mastered.

The Leadership Competencies

In addition to the Keystone Competency, I frequently heard female leaders discuss other key leadership competencies. These competencies enhance our ability to self-advocate, prove our worth, and establish our place at decision-making tables.

Self-Awareness

Are you self-aware? Most people would answer that question with something between a resounding *yes* and a *yeah, sure*. Unfortunately, for most of us, we're wrong. Tasha Eurich's book *Insight* [7] indicated that only about 10-15% of people truly are self-aware. "*Certainly, I'm one of them,*" you just thought to yourself. We all did. That's the crux of the issue.

Most of us believe that we are relatively self-aware, which is why I don't find a lot of people actively seeking greater self-awareness. Yet, self-awareness has been shown to be the greatest determinant of success or failure in business leadership.

I encounter a lot of women seeking more confidence. From our earliest memories, we're indoctrinated with the belief that most successful girls are confident. So, from a very young age, we chase it. We chase an almost intangible thing that feels constantly out of reach. We've misdefined what it really is. We've told ourselves that confidence is deeply rooted in loving who we are, standing tall in that personhood, and not caring when people don't like or relate to who we truly are.

It's the biggest fallacy of our lifetimes.

Confidence isn't loving everything about ourselves. Confidence is deeply rooted in *knowing ourselves*. It's deeply rooted in self-awareness. It's understanding who we authentically are and knowing how to adapt to feel our best in any environment. Confidence is not a take-it-or-leave-it mentality that screams, "This is who I am!" It's an understanding that we are most successful when we show up as our best selves. That best self depends on the people, places, and circumstances of each interaction.

Yet, only people who possess self-awareness are capable of toggling to people and their environment. We need to stop chasing confidence and start chasing internal self-awareness.

Internal self-awareness helps us understand ourselves better. External self-awareness means silencing the imposter in our own heads. That's right. Imposter syndrome is nothing more than a lack of external self-awareness. When we have imposter syndrome, particularly in our career, we sit in silence and internally question why we're in the room, how we got the job, what made someone think we could do the job, or question if our advice is valuable.

We question our worth at every turn. Those who are externally self-aware, however, know why they're in the room. They understand why their opinion is sought and how their voices add value because they've asked.

External self-awareness and destroying the imposter that lives inside our heads requires us to: ask how we are perceived by others and engage in conversations about our value, areas of growth, and opportunities for development.

I found that the female leaders I talked to did a lot of self-awareness building as a part of their daily habits and routines. They journaled, engaged in regular introspection, regularly sought feedback, asked lots of questions, and continued to evaluate every experience. They viewed every meeting and interaction as either a growth opportunity or a way to better understand who they are and how they could be better.

In her research, Eurich found that internal self-awareness and external self-awareness are not linked. In fact, she found that they are often inversely correlated: if one possesses internal self-awareness, one lacks external self-awareness, and if one has great external self-awareness, one lacks internal self-awareness.

This means that every woman, and frankly everyone, has work to do to grow in self-awareness. We can all continue to learn, grow, and deepen our understanding of who we are and how we are perceived by others. After all, it is a significant determinant of success in leadership.

Resilience

I consider myself an expert on resilience not because I've done some sort of ground-breaking research or studied it for an extended period of time, but because I've had to live it. If anything, I'd make an excellent participant in a study on resilience. Most of the female leaders we talked to would, too.

Regardless of the industry or profession of the women we talked to, each of them had a moment, experience, or season in their career that they could easily name as pivotal to their trajectory. In each instance, these moments were significant challenges in their jobs, careers, lives, health, personal relationships, or businesses. These women, myself included, faced a fire. Instead of figuring out a way to avoid it, they walked right through the fire and then used it to propel them into something greater.

That's the misnomer about resilience. People think resilience is merely enduring life's challenges to survive. That's not resilience at all. If it were, we'd all be resilient. Resilience is encountering challenges in life, facing them head-on, learning and growing from the experience, and then using it to propel you forward in your life or career. Resilience is almost spiteful. It's a mindset that says, "I see you, challenge, and I will be successful in spite of you."

We found that these successful female leaders looked at challenges like job loss, career change, bad bosses, bad companies, health issues, life challenges, bias, discrimination, racism, etc. They looked at those challenges and determinedly ran straight at them.

When people told them it couldn't be done or dared to use the word *impossible*, they replied, "Watch me." Those moments weren't just great triumphs in their lives. They were massive growth opportunities. These women used that growth to go on to do bigger, better things.

Women on the career ladder face more challenges than men. We encounter systemic barriers that our male peers do not, in addition to all the other things life throws at us. We can attempt to run and hide from them, but they're always there waiting for us, holding us back from our full potential.

The only way to eliminate them is to face them head-on, to run straight through the fire. We have to develop the wherewithal to face challenges, courageously walk through them, and intentionally learn and grow from them.

Courage

During an interview, I asked a senior vice president of an insurance company what one piece of advice she would give aspiring female leaders. I was surprised when her response was, "Take risks." When I went back and reviewed all the interview data, I was shocked to find that the theme repeated over and over again. The stories of female leaders were filled with choices to take big risks and those risks paid off.

When I looked at this data and then consulted the research on risk-taking behaviors and risk tolerance among men and women, I would have easily guessed that women are more risk-averse. I would have lamented that women are not inherently great at taking risks, mostly socialized to be careful, avoid pain and danger, and seek protection. As a result, women tend to take fewer risks in their lives and careers. I'd continue to explain that men were socialized for risk from a young age. They're lauded for testing the waters, making bold moves, and going for it. Their inherent lack of risk aversion shows up in their careers and their ability to self-advocate. They have a competitive advantage in the workplace and an overall willingness to ask for what they want and attempt hard things.

But then I read a new study in the *Psychology of Women Quarterly* called *The Gendered Consequences of Risk-Taking at Work: Are Women Averse to Risk or Poor Consequences?* [8] The authors argue that it's not risk tolerance that impacts gender equality in the workplace. They found no evidence of gender differences in initial risk-taking and the anticipated consequences of such risks. What they did find is a contrast in consequences where men reported more positive consequences, translating to a higher likelihood they would take the same risks again. They posit that women avoid risk-taking not because they are averse to it, but because there are fewer rewarding outcomes from those risks.

Both things can be true. I frankly believe they are. I believe there is bias and inequality in risk-taking outcomes in the workplace. That disparity is likely limiting women from taking risks. I also know that men and women are socialized differently around risks. Men and women assign different levels of danger for the same behavior.

For example, only about 14% of skydivers are women, but that doesn't mean that women are averse to risk. When you consider that a pregnancy is twenty times more likely to result in death than a skydiving adventure, you begin to see that the data on risk-taking is complex.

What is critical for women is to understand that we may have built-up negativity bias around risk-taking, particularly in the workplace, and our male peers have less aversion to it. Our outcomes might be different, too. Men might have greater success asking for a raise or calling out bad behavior from a colleague. While women might not have success asking for a raise and may experience retaliation for a callout.

Does that mean we demonstrate less risk-taking behavior? Not necessarily. It means we need to work to overcome our bias toward risk-taking and address the bias related to the outcomes.

Intuition

Listen to your heart. Believe in that inner voice. Don't ignore what your gut tells you. It all sounds like a bunch of bologna. Yet, every female leader I talked to said something to this effect. They advise women to listen to this intangible feeling that comes from somewhere in the middle of our bodies. When I identified this theme, I wondered what I was going to do with this finding. I was certain there was no data on gender differences related to trusting one's gut. It turns out I was wrong.

Intuition can be defined as what happens when the brain leverages past experiences with external information to make a decision [9]. The processing of this information happens so rapidly we are often completely unconscious of it. We feel it but can't point to why. Both men and women can be intuitive, but society has socialized us to value the traits necessary for intuition in women more so than in men. I believe that women are more in tune with other people's emotions. We're socialized that way. We also tend to look at people when they're talking to them and prefer face-to-face communication more than our male peers. As a result, we pick up on subtle, non-verbal cues. We're sensitive to body language and try to read what people aren't saying. I think that's why we're better at intuition.

Yet, the business environment is built by men, run by men, and favors the way men traditionally make decisions. Men think more linearly. They value facts, data, and reports. Society penalizes them for being sensitive or in tune with their emotions and they tend to look away when listening. They build relationships by doing and are often unaware of the minuscule changes in people's body language or facial expressions. As a result, intuition is undervalued in business and particularly in business decision-making.

Despite this, if we leverage it well, intuition can be a woman's superpower in male-dominated environments. This requires us to listen to our intuition but also to have data to support it. We can just say, "I don't know, something just doesn't feel right about this contract." We have to supply the data to back it up. For instance, "I remember last time we were in a negotiation like this and here is what happened…" or, "I was watching so-and-so's face when we were discussing the terms and I saw his body language change and smile disappear. I don't think we have it right yet."

That not only makes the case for why we are valuable but also makes the case for why we bring a unique and necessary skill to the decision-making table. Those who do not have finely tuned intuition will become reliant on your input, seek your insight, and invite you to more conversations where decisions are being made.

Every one of the female leaders we talked to referenced leveraging their skill of intuition (although they didn't call it that) to make personal and professional decisions. They also knew how to leverage it in business environments that value logic and facts.

Relationships

Maintaining good relationships and possessing good relationship-building skills seem like the most obvious competencies necessary for anyone's advancement. Frankly, it is. People are more likely to help you, advocate for you, speak on your behalf, stand up for you, or even recommend you when they have a relationship with you. However, building relationships, particularly with male peers, can often result in mixed messages.

It's no secret that the #metoo movement and #timesup have made well-intentioned men a little gun-shy about being in private conversations or meetings with women. This makes it difficult for women to intentionally build relationships and meaningful connections with male leaders. But we have to keep trying.

We also have to help the men in our lives understand what they can do to support women in the workplace (and in life, parenting, home, etc.). This goes back to self-advocacy. We have to ask for what we want. We have to explain the behavior we need from men so they can be successful allies. The truth is, there are not many great resources truly directing men on how to be great allies for women in the workplace. They think having coffee with women or having females on their team makes them an ally. We all know that's not it.

This is not just about building a cadre of male allies though, this is also about women. I want us to approach it differently. So much of the push is for women to find other female mentors to help them thrive in their careers. That's a great goal, but I think women need to take responsibility for identifying professional women who are junior to us, seeing something in them we want to grow, and intentionally tucking them under our wing to support and encourage them. We have to take responsibility for supporting the women who come behind us, too.

Growing up, I always had way more guy friends than I had girlfriends. I would lament that girls were catty and dramatic. I didn't trust them. In college, I joined a women's organization, a sorority, and my impression of women completely changed. Female relationships are powerful and important. They're necessary to our success and we must make intentional efforts to build our own bullpen of fierce women around us.

I asked every female leader that I talked to who helped them along their career journey. I was struck when many of them couldn't point to specific people. Instead, they merely mentioned some people they had called for advice once or twice, or a boss or two that supported them. It was inspiring that they had overcome all their obstacles almost entirely on their own.

However, it was also disheartening to recognize that we, as women, failed them. Despite this, as I talked to some of our younger female leaders, I discovered a major shift. These women could easily point to handfuls of women who had supported them, encouraged them, recommended them, spoke on their behalf, and pushed them to go for new opportunities.

That's the world we need to create, one where women are pushing and supporting each other up through the glass ceiling.

Communication

If you know anything about feminism or gender bias, you know that women are penalized most often for communication. Men are rewarded for being honest, to the point, assertive, and decisive. These are considered top leadership traits in men. Yet, when women exemplify these same traits they're seen very differently. Some people use bad words to describe these same traits in women. So how do we succeed amidst this hypocrisy?

I heard a lot of stories about communication from the female leaders I talked to. Time and time again they talked about learning the hard way how important communication is in the workplace, particularly when you are a woman. We have to learn how to rectify the difference between communicating authentically and communicating authentically in a way that others can hear the message. Communication, good communication actually, understands that the only way it succeeds is when the receivers of the message hear it the way the sender intended them to hear it. For women, that takes a little bit more thought and intentionality.

As a young professional, I struggled with this concept. Why couldn't I just say what I was thinking, the way I was thinking it? After all, I was being my authentic self. Over time and due to mounds of feedback, I discovered that people perceived me as too abrasive, too honest, and too intimidating. I learned how to deliver messages that would get my point across without feeling like I was sacrificing who I really was or what I believed. It's a delicate balance and you don't always get it right.

There are countless times that I remember walking away feeling terrible about what I had said and how I had said it. There were other times that I was mad at myself for not sticking up for my cause more, not standing my ground, or not calling out inappropriate comments. But each one of those moments, those mistakes, got me closer to learning how to communicate effectively as a woman.

The line between when we speak up and when we don't is different for each of us. We have to learn and test where it is so we know when we should speak up and when we should let it go.

Above all, learning how to communicate (and build relationships) are both significant skills. However, they're foundational to every role, job, and identity. They didn't feel like a "female" leadership competency more than just a foundational leadership competency. Regardless, they're integral to success in leadership and in life.

These competencies are what stood out when I talked to successful female leaders. As I began to share these findings and test how they would resonate with women, I learned how underdeveloped they really were in so many of us. Furthermore, as I began to teach them, I started to see how critical self-advocacy was. More than anything else, everything I was teaching hinged on that singular competency, self-advocacy.

I set out to write a book about all seven competencies. About a third of the way through, I said to my coach, "My self-advocacy chapter is like four times longer than all the others." It was there that she recommended the book be about self-advocacy. If that's what was really the most important, then that's what the book should be about.

Self-advocacy is what it takes to shatter glass.

It is the competency that women need to master to climb the corporate ladder, ascend to leadership, become valued voices at decision-making tables, and create the lives they dream of for themselves, their career, and their relationships. The other competencies are merely *how* you self-advocate.

As much as I wanted to write this book about the seven competencies and share the stories of the female leaders who helped me discover them, I found that where we must begin is self-advocacy. An in-depth analysis and exploration of all seven competencies is another book for another day.

Self-advocacy is what it takes to shatter glass.

Chapter 2:

This Is An Inside Job

The 7-10 split in bowling is widely considered the hardest shot in bowling. This split is when a bowler has knocked down every single pin except for two pins in the back row and at opposite corners: the 7-pin and 10-pin. Strategically, a bowler should throw the bowling ball hard enough to make one of the pins ricochets into the other so they both get knocked down. For most novice bowlers, that strategy seems like wishful thinking. As a result, they often opt for one pin or the other, surrendering a spare for the frame due to their belief that it's just too hard.

Gender equity and equality are like a 7-10 split.

In one corner, we have the necessity for women to operate within a system that consistently creates obstacles that hinder their ability to succeed. We're forced to play the game or get ostracized and labeled difficult. So, we smile, work extra hours to prove our competence and skill, ignore the passive-aggressive and inappropriate comments we're subjected to by male colleagues, get our ideas stolen in plain sight, and face constant interruptions. Yet we keep playing the game. The only other option is not being in the game at all. We want to lead. We want to climb the ladder, so we play a game that is seemingly unfair.

In the other corner, we have the action of dismantling the patriarchy and systems of oppression in corporate America. The women in this corner have had enough of playing the game and have actively decided to lunge full speed into tearing the systems apart. They're the brilliant minds behind movements like #metoo and #timesup. At every turn, they call out bad behavior, unfair and unequal expectations, and misogyny. They refuse to play a game that's unfair and instead, work tirelessly to build a new game where men and women are equal. They are the individuals who change the game instead of playing the game as it exists.

Achieving gender equity and gender equality feels like a 7-10 split with two priorities in opposite corners. Doing both seems impossible. Inevitably, people choose one corner or the other and throw that ball as hard as they can. But while making a 7-10 split is hard, it's not impossible. You can knock down both pins with the same ball.

Part of the formula for women to succeed requires serving competing priorities at the same time. It is our proverbial 7-10 split.

Over the course of my personal experience and the time I spent interviewing female leaders, I discovered that there is one thing that dramatically hinders our ability to make significant progress: the necessity to straddle two competing priorities at the same time: dismantling the patriarchy while simultaneously participating within it.

I was recently thumbing through the pages of a magazine released by my city's business journal. It recognized 250 state leaders in business, marketing, government, non-profits, law, etc.

As I thumbed through the pages, I was disheartened to discover pages upon pages of white men.

Don't get me wrong, there was a sprinkle of diversity within those pages, but it wasn't nearly enough. I was frustrated, but also not surprised. Is there a lack of diverse talent in my city or are the leadership and talent pipelines of companies here that white and male? Are feeder colleges and recruiting tactics not attracting diverse talent to the area? Or is there a lack of opportunity for diverse populations to be mentored, prepared, and funneled into a pipeline for leadership?

Regardless, systems of oppression are actively impacting women's abilities (and all marginalized and underrepresented identities) to advance, take on leadership, and impact meaningful change within these systems. Until we fix these systems, I will continue to thumb through pages of white male leaders with only a sprinkle of diversity.

In order for gender equality to become a reality and for women to be equally represented at every table where decisions are being made, we have to dismantle the systems of oppression that prevent that from happening. That means dismantling the patriarchy: the systems of oppression that fundamentally exist in business, politics, non-profits, and education.

I know I've got some nerve to say this in a book that was supposed to be about women's leadership and shattering glass ceilings. But isn't shattering glass and dismantling patriarchy the same thing?

As you read those words, you might be thinking, "How do you even do that?" That's a big question. There are lots of varying opinions on what it would take to do that, from policy and elected officials to education and conversations, and everything in between. Unfortunately, it's all of those answers and not a single solution.

Where I choose to make an impact is making decision-making tables more diverse and helping more women shatter their own glass ceilings. I believe that more women in decision-making is where we start. Because of this, I'm committed to helping women figure out how to get a seat at those decision-making tables. I'm committed to breaking down the systems of oppression that prevent us from getting there.

We cannot, however, dismantle the patriarchy from the outside. This is an inside job.

We are not a novice attempting to execute a 7-10 split. This isn't a situation where we can choose one or the other. We cannot either work within the systems of oppression or dismantle it. We must do both. We can't ignore one opportunity because it feels difficult or unlikely to be achieved. Both are possible.

This might seem counterintuitive because how can you support the system you're trying to destroy? This is the fundamental question I believe hinders our success. We think we have to pick sides. When we oversimplify a complex problem, we become paralyzed attempting to find a solution when no simple solution can be found.

Systems of oppression are complex, and so is the web of male power that has held predominant control of American business for centuries. The solution is not a simple this or that. The solution is to do both at the same time: work to advance within the systems of oppression knowing that our advancement, and the advancement of many others after us, might be the only way to blow the whole thing up.

It's the Trojan horse of the 21st century. This is a situation where we must simultaneously engage in both efforts. We must throw the proverbial bowling ball as hard as we can and hope that the two things ricochet off each other.

Why Didn't It Work Before?

I am not the first person to suggest that this is the solution to the gender equity problem, or at least part of the solution. So, if I'm *not* the first person to suggest such a thing, why have we not been successful yet? That's a big question with an even bigger answer that I cannot address within the pages of this book alone. There are plenty of scholars who have attempted to answer that seemingly simple question.

I believe the patriarchy and other systems of oppression are like a 75-legged stool. When one leg is cut off, we celebrate a victory for our cause, yet the stool doesn't fall. In fact, it's still perfectly stable. From the 19th Amendment [10] to Title VII [11] and Title IX [12]. From Shirley Chisholm [13] to Kamala Harris [14], and all the little wins (and losses) in between, we believe we are making significant progress toward equity. Yet with each of these victories, we only watch a single leg of the stool fall. Our strategy has been to knock a leg off one by one, so we knock off a leg and move on to the next. Yet, the system regenerates. As we become distracted by a new cause, an old one rebuilds. We didn't fully kill it the first time.

Take Roe v. Wade as a prime example. The landmark decision has given women choice and bodily autonomy for decades. It's allowed women to make personal decisions with their partners, healthcare team, and religious advisers. It gave women freedom in their own bodies. As we pivoted to other causes, the stool began to regenerate, and rebuild, and in 2022 the right that was afforded to women for decades was stripped away with the Dobbs decision. Now the focus returns to that cause and averted away from another.

Regardless of how you feel about the issue, the point is clear: this is how systems of oppression work. They keep the oppressed running around like a cat chasing a laser pointer, focused, but dodging around as the target constantly moves.

The patriarchy, just like any other system, benefits a small portion of the population by oppressing the rest. It's a stool of many legs that cannot be destroyed or dismantled by taking out a leg, one by one.

Divide And Conquer

Julius Caesar is noted as the creator of the political and military strategy known as Divide and Conquer. In modern society, it's become a catchphrase that describes a way to approach a problem: break it down and have different members of the group solve different parts of the problem simultaneously.

My husband and I use this phrase frequently to describe our weeknight obligations of shuttling our two children to overlapping commitments, practices, play dates, and school events. We divide and conquer, each taking a child to their obligations, and reconvening at the end back at home.

However, the meaning of Divide and Conquer has a much darker meaning. It's intended as a method to gain and maintain power divisively. It's a strategy where large enemy forces or opposition groups are forced into smaller sub-groups and are thus easier to control. In politics, it's a strategy used to break down relationships and unity between subjugated groups struggling for justice, freedom, or liberation, in an effort to maintain the status quo. In essence, groups fighting to overthrow those in control are weaker when they are split apart, fighting with each other, and focused on different things instead of working together to fight the real oppressor.

The patriarchy keeps its own destruction decentralized, making it harder to dismantle. It benefits when seeds of distrust, jealousy, and division are sown because then we fight amongst ourselves. The systems of oppression continue doing their job of maintaining the status quo. What's scarier is that most of the time, we don't even recognize that it's happening. It's so subtle and discreet that the divisiveness can often feel like support.

The Employee Resource Group

A quick internet search of "why employee resource groups are important" will produce an abundance of articles touting their necessity in a diverse workplace. Employee Resource Groups (ERGs) are groups of employees who join together based on shared experiences or identities. They're generally based on providing support, connection, and a sense of belonging in an effort to improve an organization's culture of inclusion. In addition, they work to improve the retention of employees who have an identity that is underrepresented in the workplace. They're often employee-led but supported by organizational leadership.

Organizations that have ERGs often begin with a group for women. Some organizations only have a Women's ERG. I won't dispute the benefits. They do provide an opportunity for women in the organization to connect with one another and build a sense of belonging, create mentorship, or find support. Yet, they often give the impression that they give women a collective voice to advocate for the things they need, impact change, and dismantle the bias or discrimination that might exist within the organization. *It's a mirage.*

Women's ERGs wield no actual power. They're often minimally funded and casually attended by organizational leadership. They futilely attempt to empower their female members, create male allies, and fight for a better work environment for women. In many instances, it's in vain. What they are able to achieve are small, often performative changes to the workplace environment: a breastfeeding room, a conference for female employees, a women's mentoring program, or a Women's History Month speaker.

These solutions do nothing more than placate female employees. They don't help women advance and they don't provide them a seat at the table where real business decisions are being made. They don't make them valued members of the leadership team. They don't help women ascend into leadership faster or easier.

Couple this placation with the competition for funds and attention of company executives, against the other company ERG groups, and these groups are seemingly moot. They fail to advance the true common purpose: meaningful change, more diversity at the table, and dismantling the systems of oppression that disproportionately benefit men, particularly white, straight, Christian, cis-gender men. They've effectively "divided and conquered" us and made it look like a *gift*. They've split us apart, pitched us against each other to compete for resources and attention, and minimized our power and ability to push or demand real change.

Look, I love women's groups. I think they provide a safe space for women to find support, connection, and development.

However, if we think that women's groups are going to get us closer to dismantling the patriarchy, getting a seat at the decision-making table, or impacting real cultural and systemic change in business, we're wrong. It's the *wrong work*. That work doesn't move us forward, it just keeps us busy and divided. It gives the illusion that movement is being made when nothing at all is changing.

This Is An Inside Job

If you're feeling a bit deflated after all this, don't lose heart. Herein lies the crux of the issue. Winning feels insurmountable and even when we feel like we might be gaining ground, it turns out we're either losing ground somewhere else or we're being had. I don't think the choice is any clearer regarding how we proceed. We must operate and exist within a system of oppression, while simultaneously attempting to unravel it.

The challenge is that the system only begins to unravel as we begin to achieve greater equality in leadership roles. When there are more women at the decision-making table, we can impact decisions about the things that are holding us back. *We unravel more of the system as we shatter more glass.* It's never been more important for women to succeed. When we do, we pull another string from the tangled web of patriarchy.

In this, we're forced to grapple with our own self-preservation and advancement while simultaneously carrying the futures of the women who will come after us in our hands. To be honest, I don't know if I have all the answers. In fact, I'm certain I don't.

What I do know is this: The more women I can help ascend into leadership and shatter glass ceilings, the more women that will be in the room where decisions are being made. The more women that I help understand what the successful female leaders before us did to rise, the more of us that can rise, too. In doing that, I believe that we will carry that torch forward.

We will do all we can to help more women rise and shatter glass. We will create more space for more women, more diverse voices, at more decision-making tables. But we can't do that from the outside screaming on the streets, protesting change. *This is an inside job.*

Chapter 3: Good Girls

As little girls in American society, we are taught to be "good girls." We are conditioned to refrain from demonstrating anger, allow people to violate our boundaries, and bury our own needs in exchange for pleasing people and helping others. As young girls, we take on these traits because they are rewarded in our families and in society. Being a good girl requires us to play nice, take care of others, and participate in activities that require collaboration, teamwork, and sharing. Friendship, niceness, and cooperation are prioritized. We play dolls, participate in tumbling, cheer, dance, Girl Scouts, and give near strangers hugs as greetings because that is what is expected.

Competition is conditioned to be seen negatively. We're socialized to avoid bragging or talking about our accomplishments in favor of being modest, humble, and demure. Talking about one's accomplishments or greatest qualities is perceived negatively by other women. We're rewarded for behaviors that show collaboration, nurture, support, and advocacy for the people on our teams, in our families or friendship circles, or leaders we admire. Being a good girl means sacrificing our own needs and boundaries to care for and help others. As a result, we generally turn our worlds upside down and ourselves inside out for others.

Now, I'm not positing that these qualities are a bad thing. In fact, they are extremely valuable and make women great servant leaders, people developers, and mentors. This traditional conditioning allows us to add immense value to teams and workplace culture. As women, we fiercely advocate for our friends and those who work with and for us. Mothering, nurturing, collaboration, care, and compassion are the characteristics generally expected of women. We are supposed to care about others far more than ourselves.

But being a good girl comes at a price. From a young age, we're taught that our worth is attached to sacrificing our own needs to tend to the needs of others. We are uncomfortable telling someone no, setting a boundary, or expressing how we truly feel. We're taught that doing so would be rude. The messaging is clear: being perceived as helpful and polite is far more important than our own needs or feelings. We appease, go along with, and generally avoid conflict. We become laser-focused on how we appear to others and maintain our good-girl persona.

I remember vividly in second grade art class speaking up for myself, only to be met with shock. Our art teacher had just handed back a significant art project where we were to draw ourselves doing things that we enjoyed. From a young age, I could color in the lines and could draw an image just by looking at it.

When our art teacher handed me back my art project with a less-than-stellar grade, I was stunned. As I looked around at my other classmates' scores for their less-than-quality projects, I was upset. I felt slighted and treated unfairly. So, I said something to the teacher. It was there, in second grade art class, at my small private Catholic grade school that I was labeled a bad kid, all because I stuck up for what felt like an injustice. I was labeled difficult, defiant, and ill-behaved. Teachers treated me with a shorter fuse. I was penalized for mistakes and outbursts far worse than my good girl classmates were. Those labels followed me until I left after eighth grade.

Advocating for our own needs and speaking up for ourselves is the antithesis of the good girl persona. This means that we rarely speak up for ourselves and our good girl conditioning leaves us deficient in critical relational skills. We don't learn how to speak up for our needs, set boundaries, or address conflict. The concept of speaking up for ourselves, advocating for our needs, asking for a raise, requesting a promotion, applying for a new or bigger job, standing up to personal harassment, or fighting for a seat at the table is not something that we do frequently, nor are particularly comfortable with. We fear the penalty of labels that will follow us around like a curse.

These deficiencies limit our ability to ascend in leadership. It impacts our families, our government, our businesses, our relationships, and our lives. What happens when women don't advocate for themselves? In women's absence, men fill the gap.

Men, converse to how women are socialized, are raised to be competitive, to elbow their way on a dog pile of other male peers for the alpha role. They're not penalized for impoliteness, speaking up, or setting boundaries. They're rewarded for it. In fact, for a man, a lack of self-advocacy is seen as a weakness.

From a young age, men are put into activities that require them to compete, stick up for themselves, and prove their worth. They play competitive sports with coveted positions reserved for the ultra-talented elite. They fight, play tag, and race. As they mature, that socialization shows up as over-confidence in their own competence and abilities.

They'll apply for jobs they're barely qualified for. They will walk into their boss's office and ask for a raise or promotion while barely batting an eye. They act assertively without a second thought, not only because they're socialized to see that behavior as strength, but because our culture values those traits in men.

The outcome? Men are getting promotions because they're asking for them (and we're not). They're getting raises, bonuses, rewards, and better work-life balance because they advocate for it (and women don't). They're sitting at leadership and decision-making tables (that they sometimes have no business being at) because they asked.

Simultaneously, we sit outside those rooms burying our anger and frustration because we're afraid to be labeled as difficult or dramatic. We're afraid to be perceived as anything but a good girl.

The Angry Feminist

There, I've said it. The f-word. The word that can single-handedly polarize an entire population. If the word feminism hits you in the feels, hang with me a little longer while we discuss how the word feminism and people's strong reactions to it are by design.

By this point, you've been confronted with some truths about being female in American society. You've seen some of what being a female means for you or the women in your life, the people they are, and the way they move through and experience the world. From early childhood, we work tirelessly to live up to impossible standards and placate everyone in exchange for positive labels such as mature, easy to work with, and well-behaved.

Simultaneously, something deep inside us stirs. It presents as feelings we can't quite name, but we know it just doesn't feel right. That sense of unease eventually turns into something more namable: anger, frustration, injustice, unfairness, inequity, slights, discrimination, and bias. We continue to suppress those feelings but the more we bury the emotions, the stronger they get. We begin to oscillate between the extremes, a type of code-switching between good girls and acting out.

I remember as a child having a shirt that read, "I love my attitude problem." What was likely meant as a gag gift aimed at my defiant behavior couldn't have been more true. Being raised in a large German Catholic family, the "good girl" expectation was clearly understood from as early as I can remember. From sitting in church or my private Catholic elementary school, to family dinner and the grocery store, I was expected to be helpful, compliant, polite, and quiet. Early on, the fire in me grew to where I could no longer switch back and forth between the good girl I was expected to be and the rage I felt inside. I began acting out.

I was sassy, defiant, and irreverent. I broke rules just to prove I could. I forged disciplinary slips sent home from school to alert my parents of my problematic behavior (sorry Mom). I sarcastically saluted teachers (I got a detention for that one). "I love my attitude problem" wasn't a funny gag gift, it was my mantra. I was unable to placate the expectations of me. I was unwilling to accept that was what I had to be.

But was my behavior really problematic or did it just not align with society's expectation of how a good little Catholic girl from a small farm town should behave?

What starts as a smolder sometimes turns into an uncontrollable fire. Eventually, being a good girl becomes too exhausting. We can no longer bury our emotions or cater to others. That fire is too intense to suppress and those internal feelings begin to spill out. We become angry, and that fire shows up in a number of ways. From disagreeing with opinions, addressing problematic behavior or injustice, being assertive, advocating for ourselves and others, and generally disregarding the societal expectations of likability and agreeability, that fire grows. We are no longer able to placate people with performative politeness.

Those around us are rarely equipped to deal with the fire inside. They don't understand how such a good girl can turn so bad. They marvel at how quickly we change. Rebecca Traister, in her book, *Good and Mad* [15], best describes how women's anger is cast: "Women's anger will be—as it has long been—cast as ugly, unappealing, dangerous, something to be shut down or jeered. Nothing, we have long been assured, is more unattractive in a woman than anger."

But why? Why is anger so bad and unattractive in women, when it is perceived as power in men?

Creating a culture that interprets women's anger as unattractive is used as a strategy to continue to suppress our outrage, social upheaval, and desire to challenge the status quo. It vilifies women who speak out and speak up, fighting for injustice and protesting for equality. Creating the trope of an angry feminist serves those in power two-fold. This trope cripples women with fear so they continue to bury their anger for fear of being labeled as an angry feminist, and it provides them with a villain when misogynistic systems are confronted.

"They're just angry feminists," they'll cry while playing victim to a group of what they label as unhinged, dangerous, and crazy women.

This vilification suppresses other women from speaking up even though their fires are raging inside. This trope of a woman gone mad is why we continue to be terrible at advocating for ourselves. We're forced to choose between likability and self-advocacy. When faced with this decision, our societal conditioning often overrides our intellect. We choose likability time and time again.

I caught myself in the trap of likability versus advocacy regularly. I was minding my words and opinions in a conversation in favor of being liked. I spend extra time thoughtfully considering my words, so as to not offend anyone in the conversation. I avoided certain topics so I didn't ruffle any feathers.

Even as I say these words to you, I'm mad at myself. I'm mad for shapeshifting into a more palatable version of myself so I didn't offend, scare, or alienate people. I'm mad that I have learned to do it so effortlessly that most of the time I can't even recognize when I'm doing it. I'm mad that the bold fireball I once was has seemingly disappeared, replaced with a version that is much more measured, careful, and intentional. I'm mad that I even have to have this conversation in a book about women's leadership. Yet, here we are.

During my research, I spoke with a female leader who was a high-ranking official at a prominent university. We had known of each other for years, but not much more than as casual acquaintances. Nevertheless, I admired her. She had done so much in her career that I, at one time wanted for myself. Everything she achieved, she did while being unapologetically herself. As we spoke, I asked her, "What is one critical lesson you learned in your career?"

Without much of a pause, she said, "I learned that you have to choose when you dig your heels in and when you acquiesce." There it was. She said the thing that so many of us are afraid to admit out loud.

No matter how much we would like to believe that we can move through the world existing as the most authentic version of ourselves, we just can't. We can't simplify something this complex. There is an element of our interactions, our conversations, and our experiences, where we have to decide if *this particular fight* is worth fighting or if we should let it roll off our backs.

I was once in Dallas, Texas, for a speaking engagement. Landing at the Dallas Fort Worth Airport, I exited the terminal with my carry-on and called for a ride-share. Ten minutes later, my driver, Wayne, pulled up in a white, four-door pick-up truck with big mud tires and a lift kit.

On brand, Texas, on brand.

Wayne pulled up to the curb where I was standing and walked around to the passenger side. Wayne was striking: an easily six-foot, four-inch black man with a muscular build wearing a snug black t-shirt, black jeans, black cowboy boots, and a white Stetson hat.

Okay, Texas, take it easy.

Wayne met me with a big bright smile, grabbed my bag, and threw it in the back seat. As I hopped in the front passenger seat he and I began to talk about a myriad of things, including his mentorship of inner-city black high school men.

At one point he looked at me and said, "You know what I tell all of them, Jessica? I tell them to be a duck, not a chicken."

I looked at him slightly perplexed because I wasn't quite making the connection of what that epigram meant.

He read my expression and continued, "Have you ever dumped a bucket of water on a chicken, Jessica?"

"No, I can't say that I have," I replied.

"Well, if you dump a bucket of water on a chicken, they get soaking wet. Their feathers absorb all the water. They look like a drowned rat."

"Okay," I said inquisitively.

He continued, "Have you ever dumped a bucket of water on a duck?"

"Obviously, that's also a 'no'," I responded.

"Well, if you dump a bucket of water on a duck, it just rolls right off their backs. You can't even tell they're wet."

Having fully connected the dots at this point, I looked at him and said, "That's brilliant."

We've got to learn to let stuff roll off our backs. We can't fight every battle, and not every battle is worth fighting. We have to make conscious choices of when we let it go and when we dig our heels in.

There is so much that happens to us where we don't let it roll off our backs. We absorb it, soak it up, and let that stuff weigh us down. Doing that fuels the rage that burns just under the surface. We carry it around our whole lives and it pops up at really inconvenient or inappropriate times. I have that stuff that I carry around too: comments people made, opportunities I missed, behavior that I allowed, mistakes I made, fights I should have fought and didn't.

If you soak up too much, it will swallow you.

We've got to be a duck more often and let it roll off our backs. We can't successfully navigate within the patriarchy and simultaneously dismantle it while also carrying around a bunch of history that we can't change. We can't absorb it all. We have to let some of it roll off our backs.

So here we are, grappling with a choice between following what society deems as acceptable for women or totally bucking the system. Fighting the fight or letting it roll off our backs. It's our greatest catch-22. How do you win?

If you're feeling defeated and wondering why you even bothered reading a book saying women might be in the worst lose-lose situation on the planet, stick with me. That's not the point here and is by no means what I'm suggesting.

Having the ability to advocate for ourselves effectively requires us to understand all of the systems that impact our ability to do so. As I've said before, those systems are intricate and robust. The patriarchy is difficult to tackle because it is a 75-legged stool. We have to understand all of the pieces at play. We have to play both offense and defense. We have to prepare ourselves to take action, understand our opponent, do the research, and know what we're up against before we head into the game. It's not going to be perfect. It will be messy. Mistakes will be made. You might even have some regret (more on regret later).

Yet, in the end it will all be worth it. How do I know? Because in the end, there will be more women sitting at decision-making tables, and not just sitting there watching the conversation happen.

They will be valued voices in the decision-making. In the end, more women will climb their ladders, ascend into leadership, and shatter their glass ceilings. In the end, one of those women will be *you.*

We have to recognize the things that are working against us. More importantly, however, we have to understand why this work is so important. I want a better world for myself, my kids, the women who come after me, and you. I hope you do, too.

Chapter 4:

We Don't Get Things We Don't Ask For

I was hired as the president of The Center for Leadership Excellence with the intention of someday taking over the business for the owner. The plan included my eventual purchasing of part of the business from him as he drifted out to retirement. I took a pay cut when taking the role because the possibility of ownership of the business was appealing. In my first year at the business, I took a great interest in not only growing the business with new clients, enriching relationships with existing clients, and new service/product lines, but I also took a hard look at where we were spending money.

On my one-year anniversary, I anticipated that the owner and I would discuss the year, the great successes we had, and all that I had brought to the business. I imagined the conversation would then warrant a discussion of pay and exploration of ownership shares. I was certain I had done all that I needed to prove my worthiness, so I requested a meeting.

He agreed to sit down and review the year after our regularly scheduled Monday morning team meeting. After the rest of the team cleared the conference room, I sat across from him at the long table.

"So, one year down. It flew by," he said as I sat there smiling expectantly.

"It did," I said.

He continued, "You've done a lot this year. You should be really proud of your work."

I continued to nod and smile.

He then said, "Atta-boy, girl," a term of endearment he often used to affirm good work with mostly female staff. I smiled more because those words were a truly positive affirmation from him. He then ended the conversation and proceeded to get up and leave. While that might be a slight overdramatization, the sentiment of our conversation was clear. He thought I did a good job and that was the end of the discussion.

I was aghast. That was it? After the year I had, all I got was a good job and a proverbial pat on the back? It wrecked me. I packed up my things to go home.

As I drove, my anger and frustration grew. How could he not recognize all of my contributions to the organization in the last year? I brought in a bunch of new clients. I was doing my job and the job of another team member on medical leave. I created new products and new services. I had enriched relationships with some of our current clients. I trimmed a quarter of a million dollars in unnecessary spending from our operating budget. I managed a move from an office we had occupied for decades.

How did he not recognize all of that?

By the time I got home, it was all I could think about. I opened my computer and started an email addressed to him. I pulled out the journal where I had been logging all of my important accomplishments over my time at the firm. I began to build a list of my top accomplishments over the last year. I shared in detail what I did, how it contributed to the firm, and what it demonstrated I was capable of. After I had formulated a list of ten items, I concluded the email with a request for a twenty-percent raise and ownership shares in the company.

We've all had these moments. The ones where we sit and emotionally type our feelings in an email to the person who we perceive has wronged us. In a way, it's cathartic. As women, what we do next is share that email or lengthy text message with our girlfriends, often with the question, "Should I send this?"

Generally, those requests are met with affirmations of the way we feel or the things we say. Yet, we're discouraged from actually sending it. If we are encouraged to send it, we overthink the sending and often dilute the strength of our words to be more palatable for the receiver.

That is precisely what I did. I sent it to some of my friends with the question, "Should I send this to my boss?" Their obvious responses were:

- "Absolutely, no way should you send that email."
- "Maybe you should tell him some of these things in an in-person meeting?"

In general, the consensus from my girlfriends was that sending the email would be committing career sabotage. They lauded my accomplishments and my audacity to ask for a twenty-percent raise but discouraged me from actually doing it.

I was dissatisfied with their responses, so I asked my husband. He read it, thought for less than fifteen seconds and said, "You should absolutely send it."

So, I did.

I hit send and I immediately regretted it. The next two hours I sat, staring at my computer, repeatedly hitting refresh, awaiting a response. I kept my phone close by in case he called. I rehearsed what I would say if he was angry for my forwardness or for the audacity to ask for the things I did. I considered what was the lowest I would accept in a raise, fully expecting the answer to my request to be a no.

Just shy of three hours later, a response from my boss came through my email. My heart jumped into my throat as I opened it and began to read. It said:

"Jessica, Thank you for your email. While I agree with all of the accomplishments you included, I feel there are a few you have missed. I have listed a few below. I agree, you've been an exceptional asset to the firm. I have processed your raise beginning next month with our payroll company and reached out to my CPA to set a meeting to begin the conversation about giving you ownership shares in the organization."

That was not at all what I expected. Eight months later, I didn't just get ownership shares in the company, he sold me the entire business.

When I talked to female leaders about how they were successful, who helped them get there, and what was critical to their success, their responses were surprising. Over and over again women indicated that they didn't have a lot of help. There wasn't some magical cadre of mentors or allies at work who invested in their success. In fact, it was the opposite.

One female leader said it best when she said, "I worked for three different men early in my career. They didn't help me succeed and in fact, I was successful in spite of them."

Repeatedly, I hear from female leaders that you must learn how to advocate for yourself. You have to learn to speak up for what you need or want in every little nook and cranny of your existence. If we don't ask for what we want, it's unlikely that anyone else will.

Consider how our inability to advocate for ourselves shows up in our lives. Have you ever been to a restaurant and received food that was the wrong order or tasted bad and didn't send it back because you said, "it's not a big deal?" Have you ever been mad at someone or frustrated at a situation and when you were asked if you were okay you responded, "I'm fine?" Do you have presents that you've received sitting in a dark closet unused because you don't like them, got a duplicate, or something didn't fit? Yet you can't or won't tell the person who gave it to you, that it was wrong? Have you taken on more responsibility at work but haven't asked for compensation or a title change that represents those additional responsibilities?

I think by now, you get the idea. There are lots of places where we have opportunities to speak up for ourselves and don't. These are just little examples in our personal lives where we don't speak up. If we looked at the moments in our careers that are similar, we'd likely find a similar response of choosing to not speak up, advocate, or ask.

One could argue that there are certain circumstances when the choice to not speak up is more appropriate. In certain cases, that is true.

However, we often make the choice (or excuse) to not speak up because we perceive the repercussions of the alternative to be much worse than saying nothing at all. Let's consider these alternatives for a moment.

- You get a meal that's wrong at a restaurant and you politely flag down the wait staff and inform them. The staff promptly apologizes and brings you the correct meal and comps your appetizer as further apology.
- You're frustrated with a situation with a friend. When they ask if you're okay, you respond by sharing how you're feeling and how they, as a friend, are contributing to those feelings.
- Your aunt Martha gave you a birthday gift. You open the present and it's something you already own. You thank her for thinking of you and apologetically let her know you already own the item while suggesting you go shopping together for a replacement.
- You approach your boss and ask them to discuss your current role. You share that you've had increasing responsibilities added to your plate without additional compensation or a title change. Your boss acknowledges it and schedules time to discuss the matter with human resources.

It's clear that the alternative of advocating for ourselves is the less desirable option (that's sarcasm). While each of these examples poses an opportunity to make mistakes or potentially be perceived negatively, it is clear that we've been conditioned to falsely perceive self-advocacy as negative. We won't question advocating for people we care about, but won't consider it for ourselves.

I'm guilty of this, too.

There are too many moments to count when I have chosen to remain silent, not speak up, or wait for permission or an invitation, instead of advocating for myself. We must undo our good-girl conditioning and learn how to speak up for ourselves, advocate for our needs, and set boundaries.

Failing to advocate for ourselves shows up in our professional lives, just as much as our personal ones. We fail to ask for raises, promotions, more responsibility, better balance, and so much more. We wait to be asked. We think we'll be invited. We assume that people know our needs, desires, career goals, and expertise. We assume that the people around us are paying attention and are aware of the good work we are doing. As a result, we imagine they will save a seat for us at decision-making tables. That's the fallacy of our professional lives.

In my one-year review, I didn't advocate for myself until it was over because I was upset with the result. I waited for my boss to bless me with a raise and a promotion because I perceived that to be a much more polite option than asking for it myself. I assumed he could read my mind and would inherently know what I wanted for my career and my future. I didn't ask for it. I didn't advocate for myself in that conversation. I barely even said words!

The same thing happened in my first CEO job. I got that job because I asked for it. When I started with the company I wasn't at the leadership table. I wasn't making business decisions, setting strategy, or identifying goals. I often found myself as the recipient of those things, but only after the owners had a conversation about it.

It wasn't until I turned my frustration into advocacy that I became a part of those conversations, instead of a recipient of the decisions. I started saying, "I'd really love to be a part of these conversations next time," or, "I have some thoughts about how we could make this better. Can I be a part of the discussion?" I would call the owners and share my ideas. I asked for a seat at the table, over and over again, until they made a space for me.

We can't wait for permission to show up. We can't expect people to know what we want and make it happen for us. We can't wait for an invitation. We can't sit silent and watch opportunities, conversations, and moments pass us by.

We can't let the fear of rejection or failure stop us from speaking up. We can't let society's definition of how women should behave stand in our way of asking for what we need and want. Shattering your glass ceiling requires us to get really good at advocating for ourselves in our careers, relationships, personal lives, and everywhere.

Chapter 5:
What Do We Do About It

I can vividly recall countless instances when advocating for myself blew up in my face. There was a stretch of time when I would routinely hang up on a boss (and owner of the company) because the conversation had gone to an entirely unproductive place. His visceral reactions to my assertiveness spiraled the conversations out of control.

I also know that every performance evaluation I have ever had has lauded me for my performance, the business outcomes I was responsible for, and my overall contributions to the business. Yet, in those same reviews, I was consistently penalized for my attitude. I was too assertive, too honest, too blunt. I wore my emotions on my sleeve. I could be a little nicer. I could *smile more*.

Disagreeing with these assessments rarely did me any good. They would only reinforce the point these bosses were trying to make: I was harsh, confrontational, and difficult. What that meant was I was not behaving in the way society expects women to behave. I didn't fit the stereotype and it confronted their idyllic perception of who women should be at work.

I could also tell you stories from other women that would make you gasp in disbelief. If you can imagine it, it's likely happened, and it's likely happened to a woman you know. Frankly, most women have their own war stories whether they realize they do or not. This is particularly true if you're climbing the leadership ladder or attempting to shatter your own glass ceiling.

Butting up against resistance is a part of the journey. Failing to meet the world's expectations of how women should behave is standard operating procedure.

However, there's little use in rehashing and reliving those experiences—except to fuel our own motivation to do something about it. What is more productive, in my opinion, is learning the skills and strengthening the strategies women need to ascend. It's not the experiences but the lessons that are most worthwhile. That's what this book is for: to provide practical, tactical, and actionable strategies for women to shatter their own glass ceilings.

Along my career path, I've often been lauded for my no-nonsense communication style. My straight-shooter, tell-it-like-it-is personality has often been of great benefit when at the negotiating table, delivering hard news, or closing a big deal. People generally appreciate my candor. But I also recognize that for some people it can be quite jarring.

I shattered my glass ceilings. Yes, there was more than one. I did this by getting really good at advocating for myself. I learned how to advocate for myself the hard way. I learned through trial and error. I learned by making lots of mistakes and getting lucky a few times along the way. This is precisely why I wrote this book. Frankly, it took me too long and I'm impatient. I want to see gender equality in leadership in my lifetime. I want gender equity for my daughter. If I gave women the roadmap to self-advocacy and to shattering our own glass ceilings maybe it wouldn't take as long [16].

Self-Advocacy

Effective self-advocacy is rooted in three fundamental principles: knowing who you are, what you want, and how to ask for it. Sounds simple enough, right?

As women, we'd like to believe that we have a pretty good grasp on these things in our careers and in our lives. We might believe we are highly talented, and know who we are and what we want, but recognize we need some work on the "how to ask for it" part. The truth is that we need to work on all three.

Knowing who we are is a lifelong journey. Who we are is not stagnant. Change is inevitable because every day the world changes, the people around us change, and we learn, see, and experience things for the first time. That means the work to understand ourselves and how others perceive us is constant, daily work. I think the truth is that we will never truly know ourselves perfectly, yet having a good grasp on who we are and how others see us is a critical part of self-advocacy.

Knowing what we want is just as difficult work. Frankly, half of the time I don't even know what I want to eat for dinner, let alone what I want out of my life, my work, or my relationships. I've had more conversations about what I want to be when I grow up than I care to admit. So much of our socialization has subdued us into silent suffering. As women, we're taught not to complain. So, we don't, which means that we also don't really think about what we want from our life, career, or relationships either.

If we do consider it, we think about it inversely: what we *don't* want, what we *don't* like, and what we want people to *stop* doing. That's only so helpful as we embark on the journey to self-advocacy. It's a good first step to know what we don't want, but we have to be prepared to articulate what it is that we are asking for.

Knowing how to ask for what we want might be the hardest work. We've been socialized to believe asking for ourselves is selfish. As women, we are supposed to be caring, nurturing, supportive, and helpful. We exist for others. As a result, we don't know how to help ourselves. We will go to war for others while allowing ourselves to be trampled in the process. We'd much rather have someone else ask for us than ask for ourselves.

Unraveling that social conditioning, confronting oppressive systems, and dismantling others' perceptions isn't easy. Frankly, it's hard because we have to involve other people. Not only do we have to have enough courage to ask for what we want, but we also have to convince others that they should give it to us, too.

So, here you are. Embarking on this journey to learn how to advocate for yourself: either how to do it better or how to do it for the first time.

We do all this so that we can build the life, the relationships, and the careers we imagine for ourselves. We do this to find our seat at the decision-making table, ascend into leadership, and shatter our own glass ceilings. I've learned so many of these lessons through personal experience, trauma, study, research, and talking to women just like you and me. My hope is this next section will give you the roadmap you need to circumvent some of the proverbial *earning it* that I had to do. Enough of the age-old adage of "earning your place". I earned my place so hopefully don't have you.

Part II:

Who We Are

Chapter 6: Knowing Who We Are

I've spent much of my career working with women from a variety of age groups on communication and leadership. I've lost count of the number of times that I've been told that confidence is the issue. Society has conditioned women to believe that if we have confidence all our problems would be solved. If we have confidence we will attract the right romantic partner, get the right job, do better on exams, and more.

As a result, we go on this lifelong crusade in search of this elusive thing called confidence. Companies have made billions of dollars playing to a woman's deep-seated desire to find confidence through the way she looks, the place she lives, the clothes she wears, the person she dates, and much, much more.

Confidence often feels like the "ungetable get," the thing that we can't have, but will likely die trying to find. We marvel and idolize the women who seemingly have it, too. "She's so confident," we say with adoration, jealousy, and longing. We wish for the ability to find the confidence these women in our social media feeds seem to have discovered. But what is this all for? What does this elusive thing called confidence actually get us except some extra Instagram followers? Frankly, nothing.

Studies have found that there is no link between confidence and success. It's all a fallacy. The greatest determinant of success or failure isn't confidence. It's self-awareness. That's right, knowing who you are happens to be the greatest determinant of success. That confidence stuff? Well, it's all malarky. Okay, maybe it's not total malarky, but we should definitely stop chasing it.

Personally, I think confidence is deeply rooted in self-awareness, and here is what I mean.

I often speak about this concept with college women. In American society, we're led to believe from a young age that in order to have confidence you have to love everything about yourself. We're fed marketing with taglines that say to love the skin you're in or to feel confident in whatever you're wearing. We're told that confidence is rooted in feeling good about the way we look, what we wear, who we date, the car we drive, or the purse we carry. If we don't feel good about it, well then, we're not confident. If you're not confident, you're not successful.

We're taught that to be confident you have to love everything about who you are. Yet, confidence doesn't come from loving yourself, it comes from knowing yourself. When you know yourself, you know how to be a version of yourself that feels good. You can be a version of yourself that you're proud of.

Confidence is built *through* self-awareness.

When you have self-awareness, you know what your strengths, weaknesses, and opportunities for growth are. When you know yourself, you can focus on doing the things that you do best. You position yourself to learn and grow in the areas you're passionate about and avoid the things you're not suited for. These choices allow you to feel confident because you've set yourself up to succeed.

Do you know yourself? Honestly? Would you consider yourself self-aware? Tasha Eurich, in her book *Insight*, found that while most people believe they are self-aware, very few of us actually are. If you just had the thought, "Well, I'm certainly one of the people who is self-aware," you've just highlighted the inherent problem with self-awareness: merely thinking something is true, doesn't actually make it true (as much as our brains try to convince us).

Our brains do a lot of daily work for us without our knowledge or awareness. It's supposed to. As a result, we are not conscious of many of our decisions or motives. We don't have the ability to access our unconscious thoughts and feelings. What this means is that when we reflect on why we think, feel, or act a certain way, we don't have the ability to access the true reasons why. As a result, we tend to make up things that *feel* true, instead of accessing the intricate web of neurons within our brains that dictates decision-making. We can't access many of our true thoughts, feelings, and motives.

Essentially what this means is that we lie, a lot, to ourselves and don't even realize it's happening. The reflection or introspection we're doing isn't helping us to understand who we are and why we behave the way we do. It's likely leading us further away from our own self-awareness.

I took Strengths Finder 2.0 [17] at my first job right out of graduate school. *Positivity* showed up in my top five strengths. I wasn't surprised. I considered myself a positive person. I was an optimist, a dreamer, an anything-is-possible believer. Seven years later, when I took the assessment a second time at a new company with new-found responsibilities, my strength of positivity disappeared and was replaced with communication. Again, I wasn't surprised.

As a professional speaker, trainer, and leader, replacing positivity with the strength of communication made complete sense. I found it easy to verbalize my thoughts and present them to groups. Looking back, I realize that shift may have been for another reason.

At that time, I had been in my first CEO role for several years. I had built a team of people that I trusted and who were exceptional in their work. At the same time, my alignment with company ownership started to deteriorate. As a leader, I believe deeply in transparency and honesty. Those values were guiding tenets of how I led.

Yet, how that translated when I was under stress was unhealthy. When I was frustrated with other employees, leaders, or owners, my value of transparency would morph into complaining (or gossiping) to a core group of people, several of whom I worked with. I'd call them and say, "I just need to vent…" and then launch into an epic vent session where no one was spared. I'm not proud of these moments, and looking back, I know that so much of that venting was an effort to seek validation or feel better about myself or a choice I had made.

I was totally unaware of how toxic that behavior was to my team members. I was oblivious to how negative I had become. I had become focused on the wrong things, the wrong work, and the wrong people. It was affecting me and my leadership. At that time, my self-awareness was extremely low. I assumed positivity disappeared from my top strengths because my job had changed, but in reality, it disappeared from my strengths because *I had changed*. I was far more cynical than I had ever been.

One day after a difficult conversation, I called a co-worker and close friend named KJ to vent. Before I could launch into my epic roasting of the person I had just gotten into a disagreement with, she stopped me and said, "Jessica, you can't call me and vent anymore. It's too toxic. I can't take all the negativity."

I remember getting off the call with her thinking, "Pshh. I'm not negative." But no matter how much I tried to shake her comment, it stuck with me. It wasn't until much later, after I left the company, that I realized how right she was. I was negative. My behavior had become toxic to people in my circle, and I couldn't see it.

You see, especially in the worst of situations, our brains will make up things that *feel true* in an effort to justify our behavior or make ourselves feel better. It's an automatic act of self-preservation that our brains use to protect us from being hurt emotionally. But that unconscious behavior leads us further away from our own self-awareness. It gives us a false sense of being self-aware. After that conversation, I remember thinking to myself, "Why does she think I am being negative? I'm just venting!" Do you know what happened next? My brain, actually I, made up something that *felt true*. I found a reason to justify my behavior instead of searching for ways to be better in the future.

That's the real point of all of this. There's not a really good way to override or access the work our brains do behind the scenes. Instead of trying to crack that code, we should focus our attention on something a bit more productive.

We can take these moments and use them to learn about ourselves. We can learn how we behave in certain situations and what we can do next time to get a better outcome. We can take these moments and learn what we can do differently.

Ask What

Knowing oneself requires time in reflection and evaluation. Yet, how are we supposed to get closer to our own truth when our brains do a lot of the work for us, seemingly without our knowledge or permission? How do we avoid the unconscious actions of making up things that feel true?

Tasha Eurich suggests asking "what" questions, instead of "why" questions. *What* questions are actionable. They give us concrete things to change what we do in the future. They help us to better understand how to be better, react differently, or reevaluate a situation or person. *Why* questions allow our brains to make up stories in our mind that only validate or confirm what we want to be true.

For example, take my conversation with KJ. After I got off that call, I asked myself, "Why does she think I am being negative?" I remember making up reasons why KJ might have been more sensitive to my venting that day and lashed out with the negativity comment. I made excuses that it was because of the person I was venting about or that she was still upset about something that happened a couple of days before. I made my bad behavior and her reaction to it about her, not about me.

This is the other danger of asking "why" questions. Why questions allow us to blame other people instead of focusing on improving ourselves. It takes the blame off of us and puts it on others. That doesn't grow our self-awareness at all!

My reflection after the call with KJ helped me realize I blamed KJ for the feedback when the person the blame should have been aimed at was actually me. That deferment of blame and the inability to recognize my role in the problem didn't help me grow in my own self-awareness. It led me further away from it.

Instead, I realized we need to ask "what" questions. Following my conversation with the coworker and before I called KJ, I should have asked myself, "What might be causing me to react negatively to my conversation with that individual?"

That reflection might have helped me avoid putting my anxiety, frustration, and negative energy on KJ. It would have helped me identify how to handle that colleague in the future and perhaps get a better outcome. Here are some additional questions I could have asked myself following those conversations:

- What are some other examples in recent history where I have behaved in a similar fashion?
- What about venting is toxic or negative? What can I learn from KJ about my behavior?
- What can I do to better unpack difficult or frustrating conversations?
- What are other areas of my work or life where this behavior or attitude is showing up?

These questions help us to better understand ourselves, leading us closer to self-awareness. They're focused less on what happened and more on what I can change or adjust for future interactions.

We can apply this practice to many places in our personal lives as well as careers. I often catch myself internally asking why I said or did something. It's human nature to want to understand why something happened, why we feel a certain way, or why we did something, but we're unlikely to uncover the true reason. Those questions lead us further away from self-awareness.

Instead, lets focus on what is within our control. What we do, how we react, and how we navigate similar experiences in the future is within our control. Let's focus on what we can do differently or better next time. We do that by asking, "What…"

Self-awareness is the path to ascending in your career and shattering your own glass ceiling. That climb up the proverbial ladder takes a deep desire to constantly improve. We must focus on using every experience and every failure as an opportunity to evaluate, learn, grow, and do better next time.

I call this type of reflection, "on-the-spot introspection." It's the reflection we do after something happens. It's in the moment and dictated by an experience that requires further reflection or evaluation. This type of introspection is integral to growing your self-awareness, but you can't always control when and where it will show up. That's okay.

It's important to have good introspection skills so you can effectively reflect on experiences as they happen. When you catch yourself considering an experience, pay special attention to the questions you ask yourself. Pause and write down some "what" questions to reflect on when you have the time to.

Values

In addition to building self-awareness through on-the-spot introspection, there is work we can do preemptively to better understand ourselves, prepare to make better decisions, and react better in situations as they happen. Self-awareness begins with understanding what your personal values are.

Values are the foundation of our personhood. They are the lens through which we view the world. They are the filter that we use to make our decisions and they are greatly dependent on our life, upbringing, and experiences. These things have not only shaped who we are, but they have shaped what our values are as well.

If you want to work to build greater self-awareness, begin by getting clear on your personal values. You can value your family, friends, health, or job, but those are priorities, not values (don't worry, we'll talk about priorities later). Values are the central tenets that guide your actions and beliefs. They dictate how you see the world.

If you've been in the workforce for more than a day, you've likely been asked to reflect on your personal values. It seems like a no-brainer for many of us to understand what our personal values are, but we often do the exercise to identify our values almost mindlessly. We know that we're supposed to know what our values are, but we rarely stop to define them, consider why they are important to us, and understand how they show up in our lives.

Knowing your personal values increases your own self-awareness and self-awareness is the greatest determinant of success or failure. While having clarity on your personal values does increase your self-awareness, it also helps you to decide what is important to advocate for and what isn't. It minimizes decision fatigue because you have a better understanding of things that matter to you and things that don't.

It's not enough to just know what your values are, you must also understand how these values show up in our personal lives as well as our work. Is everything we do or say going to be perfectly aligned with our values one hundred percent of the time? Obviously not, but when our decisions are out of alignment with our personal values, they are more intentional instead of reactionary.

Here's a personal example: My core values are honesty, transparency, grit, generosity, humility, and love. You could do a quick internet search to obtain the definitions of these words and understand who I am as a person. What's more important is how these values show up in my life. These values mean that:

- Honesty: I am truthful to a fault. I lack the ability to sugarcoat things.
- Transparency: I believe that problems can't be fixed unless they're known, and things are always better out in the open. I don't possess the ability to keep secrets easily and I hate surprises.
- Grit: I see challenges as opportunities to learn and grow. I love looking at things that are difficult and scary and proving that I can do them.
- Humility: I will rarely take credit for things and am wholly uncomfortable broadcasting my accomplishments.
- Generosity: I am driven by the simple fact that if I can make people's lives better by giving them the knowledge I have, I will (even if it's deeply personal knowledge from my experiences).
- Love: I believe we are to love people, without condition or judgement, and I will fight against anything that is contrary to that.

Taking the time to define your values and how they show up in your actions builds foundational self-awareness. When you know the core tenets that guide you, you can better predict how you will show up in your life, relationships, and career. But what does any of this have to do with self-advocacy? A lot, actually. Knowing these things about myself reminds me that I'm always going to:

- Advocate for talking about the problems even when they're hard and scary.
- Push for others to tell me the whole truth regardless of how bad it is.
- Naturally push to share the lessons from my experiences so others don't make the same mistakes.
- Advocate for others when I feel like they're not being treated fairly.
- Work really hard to intentionally advocate for myself because it's not natural, innate, or central to my values.

I could continue, but hopefully you get the point. Our values help us understand who we are, how we will likely react in certain situations, and how we can best advocate for ourselves. Our values are like a magic eight ball for our life. They predict how things are likely to go.

Knowing these things about myself helps me to anticipate how I will respond in certain situations, what things might trigger me to behave in certain ways, and how I can work to override any negative behaviors or tendencies. Knowing all this allows me to better advocate for what I need in my life, relationships, and career.

My personal example wasn't just a fun way for me to tell you more about who I am. It's a road map for you to do the same for yourself. Identify what your values are. Define what they mean to you and how they show up in your actions. Those steps help you to know who you are, which is critical to being able to advocate for yourself effectively.

Take Action

If you're still working on identifying or refining your personal values, that's okay. I recommend starting with a quick Internet search for a "list of personal values." Find a list with a couple of hundred options and scan through the list. Write down or highlight any words that resonate with you, then work to pare down the list until you land on ten to fifteen words. If a word doesn't feel like it completely defines the spirit of your value, look for similar words until you find one that more accurately fits. From that point, narrow your list down to seven or fewer. Then reflect on these questions:

- How would you define this value for yourself?
- What are some examples of how this value is demonstrated in your personal life?
- What are some examples of how this value is demonstrated in your professional life?
- How would this value be demonstrated through self-advocacy?

Strengths And Growth Opportunities

In addition to reflecting on our values, we can work to understand our strengths as well as opportunities for growth. As a person with humility as a core value, I understand how difficult some of these exercises can be.

However, understanding our personal and professional strengths and growth opportunities helps us to ask for what we want and advocate for ourselves more effectively. It can be challenging to differentiate the things you enjoy from the things that you are good at because they're not always the same. Below is an exercise you can do to better identify what your strengths and opportunities for growth are in both personal and professional environments.

Start by creating a list of all your talents, skills, and interests. Put everything on the list that comes to mind. Are you really good at creating formulas in Excel and enjoy basket weaving? Put it on the list. If you have a personal passion for underwater roller skating and happen to also be a certified mediator, put those on the list. There doesn't need to be a theme to your list. Even the things you're bad at but still enjoy should go on the list.

Next, rate each item on the list based on your competency level with the item. Is your competency low, medium, or high? Competency should be defined as the ability to do something successfully or efficiently.

Now, go back through your list and rate your interest level with each item. Is your interest level low, medium, or high? Think about what you enjoy versus what you don't enjoy. Consider how much time you could spend doing the activity uninterrupted. Below is an example.

Talent, Skill, or Interest	Competency Level	Interest Level
Watercolor painting	Low	Medium
Public speaking	High	High
Leading a team	High	Medium
Running	Medium	Medium
Financial investing	Low	High
Web programming	Low	Low
Financial reporting	High	Low

Finally, look at your list and the ratings you gave each item. Those ratings tell you a story about your strengths, weaknesses, and growth opportunities. Strengths are things that you have high competence in as well as a high interest. Things that are merely high competence are skills or areas of subject-matter expertise, but I only call them strengths if you have medium to high interest in them. Things where you have low competence but high interest are your areas of growth. These are things you have the desire to improve upon. Those are things to invest time in. Lastly, the things you have low competence and low interest in. Take them off your list and stop doing them. They're wasting time you could devote to things you care about more.

While only focusing on our current talents, skills, and interests for the rest of our lives feels like a great idea, it's not a reality. Many times, there are things where we possess high competence but low interest. We're stuck doing things we don't enjoy even through we're good at them. These are places where we advocate; advocate to take them off your plate or have help sharing the responsibility. Most of us will have to develop skills we don't currently have or aren't currently on the list. We'll likely discover interests that we didn't know we had or develop new ones as we age. Self-awareness requires us to constantly evaluate what our strengths, weaknesses, and growth opportunities are and work to continually improve on them.

Weaknesses

We must be intentional about how we identify our weaknesses. Weaknesses are not something you poorly attempt to do once or twice. You are supposed to be terrible at something the first time you do it. In Geoffrey Colvin's book, *Talent if Overrated* [18], he debunks the myth that the people who are the best in the world at what they do are born with some sort of innate God-given talent, a sort of magical fairy dust that is sprinkled upon them at conception. What separates the best in the world from everyone else is *deliberate practice*. Individuals who are great at something work at it daily. They intentionally focus on areas where they have the greatest opportunity to improve. While there are limitations, overall, we can be exceptional at anything we are willing to work at hard enough and long enough.

It's not fair or appropriate for us to admit defeat without giving a task the proper effort, particularly if it is the thing that stands in the way of shattering our own glass ceilings. When we identify our weaknesses, we must be intentional about identifying the things we are truly are weak in. These are the activities that we have given time, attention, and effort to, without success. Everything else is merely an opportunity for growth.

If you don't want to grow in areas of weakness and they are not integral to your success, that's okay. We can't be all things to all people all the time. You can't be good at everything either.

I wasn't always good at writing. I failed first semester English Composition class in my senior year of high school. I went to college and majored in art. I took speech as my English prerequisite so that I never had to write another paper again. Then I went to graduate school, for a master's degree in education.

In the first class of my graduate program, I realized I had made a big mistake. The program I had just signed up for was research, reading, and writing intensive. It wasn't until I was forced to write relentlessly that I realized it was something I enjoyed and was pretty good at. Over the years, it's become a passion. I now devote time daily to reading and writing. That weakness has become a strength, first out of necessity, then out of passion.

So, don't dismiss a skill too soon.

In today's environment of instant gratification, we've become conditioned to quit things that are difficult, almost the moment we start them. We've become desensitized to the struggle that it takes to become good or even exceptional at something because we only see the final product of people's hard work on social media.

We've missed the journey, the struggle, and all the failures and mistakes that it took to get them there. We missed watching them work at something while it was a weakness. We only see it once it's a strength. Don't be lured by sugarcoating. You can be exceptional at almost anything if you're willing to put in the work. Consider reflecting on the following questions to gain clarity on your strengths, weaknesses, and growth opportunities:

- What are some things that you enjoy doing or that come easy to you?
- What do you believe you are exceptional at?
- What are things that you are not good at (and have tried on multiple occasions)?
- What are things that you desire to get better at or to grow your aptitude in?
- What are things that you don't enjoy and do not have the desire to improve at?

We talk about this more in the "How To Ask For It" section later on.

How Others Know You

Self-awareness isn't just understanding yourself more clearly but understanding how others see you. Eurich calls this type of self-awareness external self-awareness. We often don't have a clear understanding of how others see us. Typically, we reside in one of two camps when it comes to external self-awareness: we downplay how others see us or we have overinflated views of how we are perceived by others.

The Dunning-Kruger Effect [19] is a cognitive bias where people of low ability, expertise, or experience tend to overestimate their ability or knowledge. The opposite effect is often cited, indicating that high performers tend to underestimate their skills. This is scientific proof that demonstrates that, as humans, we're disconnected from our own external self-awareness and how others perceive us.

This lack of external self-awareness impacts our ability to self-advocate in a major way. For those of us who underestimate our own skills and downplay how we are perceived, we fail to advocate for ourselves where we should. We miss opportunities because we don't believe we possess the qualifications, expertise, or experience when we're probably overqualified.

Sheryl Sandberg, in her book *Lean In* [20], shared an anecdotal finding that men would apply for jobs if they met 60% of the criteria, while women wouldn't apply unless they met 100% of the criteria. While that claim was merely based on speculation, LinkedIn attempted in 2019 [21] to determine if it was in fact, true.

What they discovered is that, in comparison to their male peers, women were less likely to apply for jobs:

- After they view a job posting
- That was perceived as a step up

This underestimation of our own skills is demonstrated in much more than our job search behavior, but it illustrates an important point: we are missing opportunities simply because we aren't asking for them. We aren't taking the chance. We lack the belief that our experience, expertise, or skills are as valuable as they truly are.

When I was in the process of leaving my first job as a CEO, I greatly underestimated my own expertise. At the time, my husband and I had just adopted our second child, our son Oliver. I soon realized that the demands of travel and weekend work no longer aligned with the needs of our growing family. The owners and I had a candid conversation about the expectations and demands and determined that it was time for me to exit the company. I had a ninety-day runway before the end of my employment to job search. It hardly felt like enough.

Searching for my next position was challenging. I had spent the last five years leading a family of companies as the CEO, yet I didn't believe I possessed the necessary experience to step into a CEO role at a new company. That was the type of role that I wanted, but I didn't believe I was qualified for.

I looked at countless CEO roles, talked to headhunters, and tweaked my resume over and over again to demonstrate my abilities. Despite those efforts, I continually applied for lower-level executive jobs, jobs I was overqualified for.

Ultimately, by sheer luck or divine intervention, I landed a president role at The Center for Leadership Excellence (a company I later bought). I applied for the job on a whim and regretted it immediately afterward because I didn't believe I was even remotely qualified for the job.

I often think about what would have happened had I applied for all those jobs I didn't believe I was qualified for. My own lack of external and internal self-awareness got in the way.

That's the consequence of not knowing who we are—missed opportunities. We miss opportunities for a raise, a promotion, more responsibility, a better title, a more prominent company, an invite to a meeting, and a seat at the decision-making table. Those missed opportunities add up to fewer women in leadership, fewer women at every rung of the ladder, and lots more glass ceilings left to shatter.

Chapter 7:

Imposter Syndrome

Have you ever been in a room and thought, "How did I get invited to this meeting? I am wholly unqualified to be sitting here!" Perhaps you've looked at a job posting and thought, "There is no way I could ever get a job like that." Maybe you've said words to yourself like, "I'm a garbage sham of a human/mom/girlfriend/co-worker/boss. I do not deserve these people."

No? Just me? Cool.

Imposter syndrome can be loosely defined as doubting your abilities and feeling like a fraud [22]. It is nothing more than a lack of external self-awareness. We've failed to understand (and sometimes believe) how we are perceived by others. That doubt manifests as feeling like a phony. We doubt our worth, skills, or abilities. Imposter syndrome is a major barrier to self-advocacy. When we have it, we are less likely to advocate for ourselves.

The way you overcome your lack of external self-awareness is by asking others how they perceive you. Asking people how they see you sounds terrifying right? It may not be as terrifying as it sounds. Here are a couple of examples:

You've been invited to a meeting you don't think you belong at. It's with a bunch of really important people and you've got major imposter syndrome about attending. Instead of second-guessing your presence the whole time, try this instead. Prior to the meeting, ask your boss, who invited you, why they thought you would be an asset in the meeting. Now you can prepare to be that asset, but also have a better understanding of how your boss perceives you.

There's an internal job opening that you have your eye on. It's a step up from your current role, but it's a dream position for you. You really want to apply, but don't want to feel weird at work if you don't get it. There is another team member that is applying and you're certain they are more qualified for the role. Instead of not applying, you ask a work mentor if they think you would be a good match for the role. A pro-move would be to talk to the hiring manager about the role and how you might be a good fit for the roll before you apply.

An overload of work and life has left little time for your family and friends. You've told yourself that your best friend has got to be mad at you since you haven't called her in weeks. Instead of ignoring the conversation, you call her to let her know you're still there to support her and that she's been on your mind.

See! That's not so bad. Instead of second-guessing why we're in the rooms that we're in, we should just ask. Instead of telling ourselves stories that we suck at our job or role as a mom, wife, friend, or sister, we should ask how we're doing.

Then, once people share their thoughts we should listen, learn from them, and believe what they say. Sometimes the greatest hurdle is believing others when they tell us we're good at what we do. It's much easier to believe the bad stuff. Get out of your own head. That imposter syndrome you feel is just a lack of external self-awareness that's getting in the way of you advocating for the stuff you want in your life.

Inversely, there are some people who overestimate their abilities when they lack the experience for the role. Frankly, I do this every time I walk into the gym for a workout. I strut in with the deep belief that I am fitter and stronger than I truly am. There is nothing more humbling than wanting to puke after my fourth burpee. I'm knocked back into reality really fast.

Our bodies keep us honest, but that's not always the case when it comes to jobs, job functions, or other skills that don't require a level of physical fitness to complete. That overestimation of abilities can interfere with self-advocacy because the more we fail to meet expectations, the fewer people trust us to do the work. When trust deteriorates, people are less likely to help us when we do advocate for what we need or want. Having a good sense of how others perceive you *and* what you are capable of is important to advocating effectively.

Building better external self-awareness can be as simple as asking others how they perceive you or your skills in certain environments. Kristi Hedges, in a *Harvard Business Review* article titled *How Are You Perceived at Work? Here's an Exercise to Find Out* [23], outlines a relatively simple exercise for a better understanding of how you build external self-awareness. It's three easy steps:

1. Pick five people at work that you are repeatedly in work situations with. If the individuals know you in more than one aspect (like outside of work), that is even better. Be

sure to pick people who will be honest with you and not just feed you lip service.

2. Meet with them in person. Set expectations up front that you will be talking to a handful of colleagues. This helps determine if there are any common themes in the feedback. Be clear that you desire complete honesty in an effort to build greater awareness to your strengths, weaknesses, and opportunities for growth.
3. Ask two specific questions: What is your general perception of me? What can I do differently that will have the greatest impact on my success?

In these conversations, you should resist the urge to react, explain yourself, or ask why they didn't tell you this before. Simply listen, take notes for yourself, restate what they are saying to ensure that you have understood, and then thank them for the feedback. Once you've completed all the conversations, look for the common themes, reflect on what you can do differently, and work to adjust the way you are perceived by others.

Eurich indicates that internal self-awareness (how we see ourselves) and external self-awareness (how others see us) are not correlated. In fact, they are inversely correlated, meaning that if you have great internal self-awareness, you likely need to work on your external self-awareness. That means we all have work to do to better understand who we are and how others see us.

If you have a great handle on how you are perceived by others, you likely have work to do to see yourself more clearly. That's why self-awareness is such a critical part of self-advocacy. The work to continue to cultivate our own self-awareness is continual. It's not a concept that has a finish line.

Our Stories Make Us Who We Are

I often wonder how my career journey would look if one thing had been different. It's a rabbit hole that I can quickly and easily go down. It's a series of what-ifs related to relationships, decisions, challenges, adversity, and change. I'm not on the career path I originally envisioned for myself by any means.

In college, and particularly after graduate school, I had a plan. I had a very clear picture in my mind of what I wanted my life and career to look like. I had the steps that it would take to get there laid out in my head. I would do this and then I could do this and then I could go there and do that, then that. About six months into my professional career, I quickly began to realize that I probably had it all wrong. Six months later, my plan completely fell apart. I took a job I never dreamed of taking, with a company that was barely in existence, doing work that was nowhere near my target career. I leaped into the vast unknown. It was the best decision I ever made.

No female career path is linear, I've come to learn. After talking to countless women, at various stages in their careers, I see clearly now that the plans we make for ourselves quickly become fiction as soon we step into our career journeys.

Is this a uniquely female phenomenon? I don't have any data that tells me either way. What I know is that so many of the women that I have talked to, interviewed, and discussed their journeys with, share a similar sentiment: their path wasn't what they thought it would be. Surprisingly, that winding road we often take to get to the place we are is what prepared us to be where we are now.

During my research, I encountered a number of women who could point to a significant turning point in their careers. Whether those moments were the result of job loss, downsize, failure, personal matter, or simply a need for change, they all pointed to specific events that mattered along their career paths.

When I left my first CEO job, it was difficult. I had worked for the company for over eleven years. I was their first employee and I had spent much of my early career building the business alongside the two owners. I had not only built the company, but I had built my personal brand as a leader within the industry we were a part of. I was a trusted voice, a subject-matter expert, and a person who was deeply ingrained in the conversations driving our industry. In many ways, I had become a big fish in my pond.

When it came time for me to leave, it felt like I was starting over. I didn't have many relationships outside of my former industry, if any. I wasn't known or sought out for my expertise. It felt like a major step back. While I knew that my skills and expertise transferred easily into different industries, it was difficult to help corporate America see the value of my experience in higher education. It was a difficult blow to my career aspirations and the vision I had for my career. I felt like I had wasted the last fifteen years. I felt like a complete failure.

It wasn't until several years later that I realized how important those experiences were for my career today. Everything I experienced in that company prepared me to own, run, and lead my own successful business. That was the sentiment among the other female leaders I spoke with. There wasn't a career move they made that wasn't worth it, even when it wasn't a part of their original career plan and even if it was hard.

Now, we could debate whether those women simply made good career decisions or whether they took the lessons they could from each job, regardless of the experience. It might be a little bit of both. Regardless of what the answer is, one thing is clear.

Our career journeys are destined to be riddled with detours, delays, and potholes. They will not be what we envisioned or intended them to be. However, each of the jobs, each of the steps, and each of the experiences on your career path contains important lessons that help you to grow. Our stories and our experiences make us who we are.

I've been told a number of times to have patience with myself and my career journey. When someone says it to me, it always feels so patronizing. It feels like a more politically correct way of saying that I have to earn my place. It's that type of philosophy that only reinforces the hustle culture where if you're not working stupid hours, ignoring any semblance of a life, and burning out in a fiery blaze by the time you're thirty, then you are not working hard enough. As if the only way you can earn career success is by working so hard that you encounter a mid-life career crisis that has you contemplating opening your own bakery or a bar on a beach.

It's not about patience. We're not waiting for our time to come. The journey is about persistence, not patience. Patience is passive. It's like waiting around for someone to bless you with your dream job. Persistence is active. It's working every day toward your goal. It's understanding that every step is important because it brings you closer to the person you desire to be, the relationships you desire to have, and the career you want for yourself.

The person you desire to become is built on every single one of your stories and experiences. These stories make you who you are. Understand them, reflect on them, learn the lessons they were meant to teach, tuck the skills you acquired into your tool belt, and keep on climbing.

A part of me was ashamed I was a CEO and then I wasn't. I was hesitant to tell people about the industry I came from. I was certain they wouldn't understand my expertise and that they certainly would discount my experience. That changed when I learned to embrace my stories, my experiences, and my journey.

The real gift is to understand your own stories, the lessons they brought you, and how they have shaped the person you are. Our stories make us who we are, they help us to know ourselves, and they prepare us for every step on our winding path. This is all a part of self-awareness. It helps us advocate for ourselves more effectively.

Who We Are

Knowing who we are is the first step to better self-advocacy. We all have work to do in this area. This work is continuous because our environments, circumstances, and co-workers change regularly. Similarly, our skills, expertise, and experience evolve as we move through our career journeys, ascend the proverbial ladder, and get closer to our glass ceilings.

Working on self-awareness must be a part of our habits and routines. It must be something we persistently work on. It cannot be casual, like the reflection we do in the shower, driving to and from work, or as we lay in bed at night. That constant rehashing and replaying of the moments that we wished we would have handled differently cannot be the most significant introspection we do.

Similarly, we cannot rely on personality type indicators or other personal assessments to inform our entire self-view. Our number, color, letter, top five, or even our four-letter combination only provides a hint of who we are, what we're good at, and how to best ascend in leadership. We can't rely on these things to do the heavy lifting of self-awareness. They're merely an aid.

Write It Down

Real self-awareness work is thoughtful, intentional, and routine. Take the time to reflect on what happens at work and what it can teach you about yourself, how you lead, and where you can grow. We must regularly reflect on our values, strengths, weaknesses, and growth opportunities. It's critical to capture our feelings and emotions in the moment, as well as preemptively think about what we want in the future.

When I first started in my role as president at The Center for Leadership Excellence, my boss and the owner, Dick, asked me to start tracking my accomplishments. Dick is an anomaly in business. In his early eighties, one of his passions was teaching women how to take responsibility for their own careers. He had been in business for sixty years. During that time, a number of women worked for him, including the powerful force that is his wife, RoseMarie. It's rare that men from his generation are like him. It has been refreshing to work for him and with him during my time at The Center for Leadership Excellence.

In my first weeks at the firm, Dick gave me the task of spending five to ten minutes each day tracking my achievements and accomplishments. At first, I was annoyed. The idea of writing down what I got done each day seemed unnecessary and arduous.

Roughly two weeks into my role, he asked me how my success journaling was going. It wasn't going well.

At that moment, Dick looked at me plainly and said, "Jessica this is the problem. People have a perception that their bosses are paying attention to everything they are doing at work, day in and day out. They believe that they're aware of all the good work they are doing, the successes they're having, and how their work is contributing to the business outcomes. You're wrong."

Ooof. That hit me like a punch to the gut. He was right.

Our ability to self-advocate begins with knowing who we are. A significant part of who we are is what we achieve at work, what our work shows we have the potential to do in the future, and how our work contributes to the overall success of the business. We assume our bosses know these things. What we often forget is that while we are busy trying to get our boss to notice our good work, our bosses are doing the same: trying to get their own bosses to notice their good work, too. They're working on their own promotion and their own raise. Tracking our accomplishments is critical to the "how to ask for it" part of self-advocacy.

As you begin recording your accomplishments daily, don't just make a list of what you did. You want to record not only what you did, but:

- What it shows you are capable of or have the potential to do
- What skills or abilities it demonstrates
- How do those things contribute to the overall outcomes of the business

Write down anything that you have accomplished each day, even if it is seemingly meaningless or doesn't feel critical to the business. For instance, take an accomplishment like getting your inbox to zero. Now, zeroing out your inbox may feel like an accomplishment to you and may relieve an immense amount of stress, but it may not seem like a noteworthy success to your boss. But consider what skills or abilities it might demonstrate.

It shows that you can be organized, respond in a timely way to the needs of clients and colleagues, and are self-driven when direct business needs might be low. Reflecting not only on your achievements but what skills they demonstrate and how they contribute to the success of the business is what makes the Success Journal a powerful tool for self-advocacy. Consider these Success Journal points:

- Success: What did you achieve at work?
- Skills: What skills does this achievement demonstrate in you?
- Potential: What does this achievement show you have the potential to do within your role or the organization?
- Business Success: How does this achievement contribute to the success of the business or the overall business outcomes?

I was working with a young female leader and asked her to write down her accomplishments from the last six months. She was new to success journaling but had an impending performance evaluation and had asked for help to prepare. She came back to me with a list of big accomplishments. It was an impressive list, but it wasn't detailed enough. She had just completed managing a massive project for her department and ensured it crossed the finish line. That accomplishment was simply stated in her success journal, "Managed [project] and ensured it was delivered to the client by the internal target date."

This was a perfect illustration of why journaling daily is critical to truly capture the depth and breadth of what we do at work. What this young leader failed to capture was all the work that went into managing that project to ensure that it was delivered to the client by the target date.

This project required her to engage with multiple departments internally and several external partners. It required her to regularly communicate with the client to obtain information, provide updates, and gain feedback. It required her to engage with multiple C-level leaders across the organization on a regular basis. It required her to hold others accountable, including individuals that she did not have formal oversight over.

I could go on, but I think you get the point. The robust list of smaller achievements is a more profound demonstration of her skills and abilities. It perfectly illustrates her impact on the business and allows her to draw more powerful connections to what she is capable of. As a result, she'll be set up to advocate for more responsibility, a raise, or a promotion.

We often discount, downplay, or minimize our accomplishments as women. That's part of our good girl socialization. We're indoctrinated with the idea that bragging or touting our accomplishments makes us conceded and selfish. We must work to override this social conditioning.

Being able to successfully record and then share your accomplishments is a critical part of self-advocacy. I was lucky that Dick asked me to begin tracking my accomplishments when I started in my role at The Center. It allowed me to successfully use those accomplishments to advocate for the things that I wanted a year later. It allowed me to effectively demonstrate who I was as an employee with data and facts.

The business world is built by and still largely dominated by men. Men value logic and facts. They like to make data-driven decisions. They balk at intuition and making decisions based on feelings. But they also evaluate men and women differently. Data shows that men are evaluated based on their potential while women are evaluated on their achievements and prior work performance [24].

The combination of those two truths requires us to advocate for ourselves using data and facts. We have to show we are capable through our achievements *and then* plainly state what it means for our potential. We cannot expect people to read between the lines or draw the conclusions we hope for. Spell it out for them plainly. We'll get into how to use your success journal to advocate for yourself effectively, but we must first understand how critical it is to start recording our successes. It provides us with all the data we need to self-advocate effectively.

Part III:

What We Want

Chapter 8:
Your Priorities

A professor stands in front of his class on the first day of a brand-new school year. She gently places a large glass pickle jar on the table at the front of the room. The jar is empty and the label has been removed, but it's obvious to most people that it previously held a lifetime supply of unsliced dill pickles from a warehouse store.

The professor greets the class, then rhetorically asks, "Can we all agree that this jar here on the table is empty?" The full classroom nods in agreement, wondering what the professor has in store for them. Just then, the professor pulls a bucket from under the table containing large, smooth river rocks. The rocks are mostly the same size, but range in shape from a softball to a baked potato. They're just small enough to fit through the opening at the top of the pickle jar. Carefully, the professor places the big rocks, one by one, into the jar until she can no longer fit another rock in.

The professor looks up at the class and says, "Is this jar full?" For a moment, the class carefully considers the answer, but tentatively responds with mixed responses. Some students indicate yes, the jar is full. There is no more room for additional rocks. Other students argue that there is room, but for rocks of a smaller size. The professor seems to relish in the discussion. With a smirk on her face, she casually pulls another bucket from under the table.

In the bucket are tiny pebbles, smooth like the big rocks, but ranging in size from a dime to a quarter. The professor then begins to pour the pebbles into the jar. The pebbles roll off the big rocks and settle in the jar. She shakes the jar, causing the rocks to tumble further down, and then proceeds to pour more pebbles in until there is no room left for any more pebbles.

The professor looks up at the class and says, "Is the jar full, now?" The class resoundingly says, "Yes." The professor smiles and pulls a third bucket from under the table. In the bucket is fine sand. The professor then begins to pour the sand into the jar, shake the jar, and continue pouring the sand until there is no more room for sand in the jar.

"What about now? Is the jar full, now," She asks?

The class, sensing there is more to the exercise tentatively says, "Yes."

The professor again smiles while pulling a pitcher of water out from under the table. She slowly begins to pour the water into the jar as it fills up every remaining space in the jar.

The professor looks up at the class and says, "Now I think the jar is full." The students all nod in agreement. She then asks, "What is the point?"

A student in the back of the class shouts, "There's always room for more stuff!" The rest of the students smile and chuckle at the accurate comment from their peer. The professor smiles, congratulates the student on the clever response, and replies, "Not exactly."

Time is our most valuable resource as human beings. It is the most valuable thing we own. It's also finite. We only have so many minutes in every day and (I believe) we have a predetermined number of days here on earth before they are gone. Our time cannot be replenished or replaced. Once it is gone, it's gone.

The jar represents our time: there's only so much space in it. The rocks, pebbles, sand, and water represent what we fill our time with. The big rocks represent our top priorities. These are the things that are most important to us at that time in our lives. They are the things we devote most of our time to.

The pebbles represent things in our lives that take time and attention, but they either don't take a ton of our time, aren't as significant to us, or they represent the priorities of other people. They're likely meaningful or important to us, but not critical. They represent things like time with friends, volunteering at the school book fair, visiting a friend in the hospital, attending a meeting we may not need to be at, etc. The sand and water often represent the things we do as a part of everyday life: driving to work, brushing our teeth, paying bills, reading emails, etc.

If the professor had begun the demonstration with the sand or the water, the jar would have still ended completely full, but the contents would have been drastically different. There would have been no room for the big rocks or pebbles. If the professor had started with the pebbles, there certainly would have been additional room for the sand and the water before becoming totally full. However, there still would have been no room for the big rocks.

We have to put our big rocks in our jar, *first*. We must fill our time with the big priorities in our life, first. It's really easy to let our life and our time get away from us. We could easily fill our days with things that are represented by the sand. We could let the priorities of other people overtake our lives (people pleasers, I'm talking to you). If we're not paying close attention, our jar can quickly get filled with stuff we didn't want in there in the first place.

Knowing what we want is fundamental to self-advocacy. Knowing what our priorities are, or our big rocks, is critical to our ability to advocate ourselves. For most women, however, we don't have a clear picture of what our priorities truly are. Let me say that again, more clearly. As women, we are conditioned to be helpful, collaborative, and nurturing caregivers. That manifests as literally every woman I know does too much, takes on too much, and generally has too much on their plate. That stuff is generally what *other people* need or what.

Most of us are paralyzed by the amount of stuff we have to do on a daily basis. We're burnt out, overwhelmed, and stressed. The problem is that most of our stress is a result of making other people's big rocks our own. We spend all of our time on other people's priorities. Our jars are filled with other people's rocks.

When I say these things to a room full of women, I'm often met with blank stares and nodding heads. It's a collective recognition and agreement that we are doing too much. We're exhausted. As this head nodding happens, I can only assume that the room is collectively running through their to-do list, determining if anything on their list is actually their priority, instead of the priorities of other people.

This isn't just about the to-do list of our lives, either. It's our to-do list at work, as well. Our calendars are hijacked, and our email and phones are blowing up with requests, updates, and needs of other people. Our boss calls with an urgent need and expects us to move our work (and sometimes worlds) to accommodate it. I talk to so many women who just wish they had more time to do their actual work. Our jars are filled with pebbles and they're not even ours!

Our most valuable resource is wasting away, spent on the priorities of other people. As a result, we aren't advancing. We aren't self-advocating. We're mired down in what other people need instead of understanding what we need and want, and how to get it.

Get clear on what your priorities are and protect your time for those priorities as if it's the most valuable resource you own, because it is. This is not new information. We know that time is precious and that we have to focus on our priorities. If we know that, then why can't we do it? It's likely guilt, perfectionism, or both. You pick.

I am no stranger to guilt. I was raised Catholic. I think they have the market on guilt cornered. For women, the hold guilt has over us is pervasive and strong. We have a strong need to not let people down or disappoint people who depend on us. This translates into lacking the ability to say no when something is asked of us.

We worry that we'll let someone down or we could potentially miss out on an opportunity to network, prove our skills, build a relationship, or get in good with the boss. We say yes because we don't have a great handle on our own priorities and how much time we need to devote to them each day, each week, and each month. We keep saying yes until we're completely overwhelmed and burnt out. It happens because we're spending all our time on things that don't matter to us. They matter to other people, maybe even people we care about a lot, but they lack significance to us.

We ruminate about all the things we could possibly lose by not taking the opportunity or saying yes to a request for help. The guilt layers on as we consider how saying "no" will impact the other person, without stopping to consider how the "yes" impacts us.

Instead, let's reframe. *What do you gain by saying no?* Consider how saying no impacts you positively, instead of negatively. Let go of the guilt you feel for not helping someone else out and consider how you're helping yourself. If you've just read that and thought, "But that's so selfish," you've proved my exact point. We've been conditioned as women to perceive any act that is not for others as bad and selfish. As I say to my daughter, "Let it go, Elsa."

If you're not intimately involved with guilt, you are certainly in a relationship with perfection. Society expects women to be perfect. We spend our whole life chasing it, hoping that one day we will catch it. The pursuit of perfection, however, is a lot like a hamster wheel. It's impossible to get off *gracefully*. We say, "I'll be perfect when . . ." and we place qualifiers around where the finish line for perfection is.

As we begin to approach that finish line, we move it further away. We change the qualifiers. Our priorities become misguided. They become focused on unrealistic expectations placed on us by society or ourselves.

I often marvel at the women who seemingly have it all together. They somehow have mastered having everything we've been chasing and they make it look completely effortless. Its infuriating.

There's an episode in the eighth season of the television show *Friends* called "The One with the Secret Closet." In the episode, Chandler realizes that there is a closet in the apartment he and Monica share that he has never opened. Monica's character is a has-it-all-together, neurotic clean freak that is often portrayed as the most responsible person in the group. In this episode, Chandler becomes fixated on what's in the closet, even after Monica assures him that there's nothing to see.

At the end of the episode, Chandler finally breaks into the closet to find it piled to the ceiling with junk [25]. As it turns out, even Monica has her own chaos, no matter how perfect she looks on the surface. Deep down we know that these perfect women, just like Monica, don't have it all together. We know that we all have our own chaos.

What I have come to realize is that the women who seem to have it all together are actually the ones who have mastered the art of making their actual priorities a priority. They've honed in on the things that are most important to them in life. They've clearly defined what the priorities are and they protect the time devoted to those things ferociously. They're not perfect and they don't have it all together, they've just figured out how to focus on what matters most to them. They've perfected a tiny list of really important things.

We have to identify our priorities and then clearly define them for ourselves. Seems easy, right? You could probably rattle off six things that are priorities in life and career right now. But can you clearly define them? Further, it's not enough to rattle off words like friends, health, getting promoted, my partner, etc. We must clearly define what they are, what they mean for our lives, and how we will focus on them like it's the only thing we have to do.

If you were to ask me at the beginning of 2021 what my priorities were, I would have told you my family, my physical fitness, my career, and volunteering my time. While I think that's a good list, I've not done a good enough job defining them. We have to be able to further define these priorities so we're clear about what we should be spending our most valuable resource (time) on. Here's how those priorities could be further defined:

- My Family: I want to be present and engaged as a partner and a mom. I want to be able to take my children to school and pick them up, be present to watch their after-school activities in the evenings and weekends, eat dinner together as a family, and put my kids in bed each night. I want to support my husband as an equal partner in raising our children.
- My Physical Fitness: I want to reclaim my passion for running and regain the stamina to return to distance running for my own physical and mental health. I want to be in a place where I can, with little motivation, log twenty to twenty-five miles of running a week.
- My Career: I want to continue to conduct my research on executive women and position myself as the subject matter expert in women's leadership. I want to build opportunities to educate and speak to women about the necessary leadership skills to ascend into leadership. I want to build a brand and reputation that can transcend the brand of any company I may be associated with. I want to build a thriving company that is focused on building great leaders, and as a result, brings joy back into organizations and people's work.
- Volunteering My Time: I want to continue to serve as a court-appointed special advocate for children in abuse and

> neglect cases in Marion County. This is a way to support my community, impact children's lives, and support families in need. I want to devote my free time to causes that matter to me and that align with my personal passions of social justice, equity, and education.

These definitions leave no room to question where I should be spending my time and what I should and should say no to in both my personal and professional life. This is an example of how we set priorities for ourselves. Can you clearly define what your priorities are right now?

Our priorities can change, too. They evolve and refocus over time, but they can also change abruptly in times of adversity or significant change.

At the end of February 2021, I was diagnosed with stage 1B triple-negative breast cancer. In a single phone call, my priorities changed. I didn't have space to just tack another priority on top of my already long list of priorities. I had to re-evaluate. As I reflected on what was important to me, I made the decision to prioritize my health and my cancer treatment first and foremost.

That meant that I moved or canceled other appointments, meetings, or time with family and friends to accommodate my treatment. I knew that patients who began treatment within thirty days of diagnosis had better outcomes than patients who didn't. I was determined to say yes to every first-available appointment that I could take. I didn't want my treatment to stall because of appointments that fit with my schedule. I made the schedule work for me. I started chemotherapy twenty-nine days after I was diagnosed.

Within nine months I had completed eight rounds of chemotherapy, a bilateral mastectomy, and twenty-five rounds of radiation.

Those choices required me to scale back other priorities. It required me to eliminate my priority of physical fitness, too. Look, I tried to work out while I was in treatment. I poured myself onto a bike that goes nowhere three separate times, determined to be one of those people who works out through treatment. I even have a picture of myself, bald-headed from three rounds of chemo, sitting on my bike right before a ride. That was the last ride I took.

After my fifth round of chemotherapy, I began experiencing severe bone pain. My doctors all recommended that I try walking, that gentle exercise was often helpful to ease the bone pain. So, one day I slipped on my sandals and attempted a stroll down the block on a hot summer day. I made it to my next-door neighbor's house before I felt like I'd crumble from exhaustion right there on the sidewalk. Soon thereafter, I was put on physical restrictions following my mastectomy. It would be over eighteen months before I would work out again. Out of necessity, I was forced to reset my priorities.

I also scaled back my volunteering. I scaled back expectations at work. I put new research on hold, and I was physically unable to be as present as I would have liked for my family. There were many nights that I'd crawl into bed after my daughter came home from school and I would stay there, my kids often putting me to bed instead of the other way around. My priorities had to change. It wasn't really a choice I could make.

Sometimes our priorities change out of necessity and sometimes they change because we make the conscious choice to realign. The way we spend our time should be on purpose. We can't allow our priorities to become overtaken by the priorities or needs of other people. That makes us feel like we're failing when we're not. What we need is to realign our priorities.

"But I like helping people, especially the people I care about," says practically every woman, everywhere.

Look, I'm not suggesting that you can't be helpful and caring to others while also self-advocating. If being present to help the people in your life is a main priority, then let it be a priority. Let's just be intentional about it. Clearly define for yourself the people you are there to support and how you are willing to support them. When we're not clear, we can fall victim to saying yes to everything.

Be intentional. Time is a precious resource. Let's make the way we use it a choice, not the result of other people's choices. When you know what you want, you can self-advocate best. That means clearly defining your priorities so that you understand how to self-advocate.

Chapter 9: When Our Choices Are Aligned

When I was in my twenties, my career was one of my biggest priorities. I had aspirations of being a chancellor at a university one day. As I became more acquainted with the landscape (and politics) of higher education, I pivoted to business leadership. Regardless of what type of company it was, I knew I wanted to be a leader. I wanted to climb the proverbial ladder and ascend into leadership.

As I took my first big kid job after graduate school, I began prioritizing my career. I worked constantly. I traveled over 200 days a year. I said yes to extra work, attending conferences, and extra travel every chance I got. As a result, I missed girls' weekends, reunions, weddings, funerals, parties, holidays, family gatherings, and visits with friends. My personal relationships and romantic relationships suffered, yet I kept working.

I never felt like I was missing out on anything because I was focused on my biggest priority: climbing the ladder into leadership as fast as I could. And I did. I climbed the ladder, fast. I climbed from coordinator, to director, to vice president, to CEO. I shattered my own glass ceiling before I was thirty-five and I never had any regrets about it.

That's what happens when the choices of how we spend our time are aligned to the things that are most important to us. It's easy. We don't feel like we're missing out on anything. We don't feel burnt out. The focus on what is important to us gives us energy, focus, and enthusiasm for the tasks. If you don't feel that way about how you are spending your time, it's likely because how you are using your time is not aligned with your priorities. You're spending too much time on things that aren't a priority or are the priorities of other people.

It's time to reevaluate. Start by making a quick list of the things that are important to you, off the top of your head. Next, go through and estimate what percentage of your time you are spending on those things. It's okay if it doesn't add up to one hundred percent. In fact, it probably won't. Then, ask yourself the hard questions: Is this what I want to be spending my time on? What would I prioritize right now, if I could? Do these priorities match how I currently spend my time?

After some focused reflection, you'll probably have a better answer of where you need to readjust. Understanding what your priorities are helps you to better advocate for yourself, the way you spend your time, what you chase, and what you should get good at saying no to.

Without priorities, we fall victim to shiny objects, emotional decisions, and the efficacy of other people's begging. We end up misaligned in our priorities, which makes us grumpy, burnt out, stressed, and with major FOMO (fear of missing out). Knowing what our priorities are is a critical part of knowing what we want. But it's also an important part of feeling good about how you spend your time.

Once we identify our priorities, protect them like they are more precious than diamonds. This is oftentimes where we fail. We can clearly define what our priorities are, but we often lack the resolve to protect them. Set boundaries to protect the priorities in your life. Boundaries are a key part of self-advocacy.

Shortly after I became CEO for the first time, my husband and I adopted our first child, our daughter Emery. When Emery came into the world, in a blink of an eye our lives changed. Slowly the travel, the work, and the time away from home didn't feel good. I started to realize that while I loved my title of CEO, I loved the title of Mom much more. At the time, I didn't have great clarity or the right words to describe this phenomenon. So, I did what most of us do. I kept trudging along.

I slowly became more and more discontent. I liked the travel less. I found excuses to not go to things, and I hated being away. I did this for three years until we adopted our son. Two weeks after Oliver was born, I was pulling into the airport parking lot chugging the world's largest Diet Coke and hating myself for it (the travel, not the Diet Coke). When I returned from that thirty-six-hour, west coast trip, my husband took one look at me and said, "This isn't going to work." He was right.

My priorities and my family's priorities had changed. The work was no longer joyful. It felt like a sacrifice. It felt like *work*. My priority was no longer climbing the corporate ladder as fast as I could. My priority was now being present and engaged with my family.

That change in priorities required a reset of boundaries, too. In a way, it helped me correct all the mistakes I had made early in my life and in my career. It helped me become more protective of my priorities and set better boundaries to protect them.

Because now my priority was to be present and engaged with my family, I had to set boundaries to protect my ability to do that. I wanted to walk my daughter to and from school every day. I wanted to be focused on my family in the evenings for that tiny sliver of time between work and bedtime. So, I created boundaries to protect that time. I blocked my calendar in the morning and mid-afternoon to protect drop-off and pick-up from school. It's a fifteen-minute appointment on my calendar but protects that time from being stolen for the priorities of other people. I don't schedule evening calls for volunteer responsibilities unless they're after 8 p.m. I now make my visits monthly for my court-appointed special advocacy (CASA) cases while my daughter is at sports practice. I say no to things that interfere with those carefully drawn boundaries.

I try had to not let people take advantage of or cross over those boundaries, either. The minute you let someone cross a boundary *is the minute that the boundary disappears*. If you allow someone to take that time away from you, they'll get the impression that the boundary isn't real. As a result, they will continue to step over the boundary line.

Taking a hardline approach to protecting your boundaries helps others learn what is important to you. They slowly begin to learn your boundaries and make moves to accommodate or respect them. Recently, I offered to meet with a staff member during school pick-up time. It was critical that we meet, and our availability wasn't really aligning well. When I offered the 2:20 p.m.

to 2:50 p.m. spot, their response was, "Are you sure?" Protecting my boundaries taught my team to respect them, too. If you don't protect it, they don't respect it.

A female leader once shared with me that she was struggling with boundaries. She liked to work out during her lunch hour and had taken steps to protect that time by blocking it off on her calendar. Her challenge was that she was constantly encountering requests for meetings that overlapped with her workout time. She felt like she couldn't say no. The boundary she set wasn't being respected, and as a result, it essentially disappeared.

I asked her to start declining meeting invitations that overlapped with that time or sharing with the host that she would have to leave early or come late to the meeting based on how it bled into her workout time. The change didn't happen overnight, but slowly she was able to reclaim her workout time more often. Her colleagues and her team started to see that specific time was important to her. As a result, they worked to accommodate it.

Look at your priorities list. Ask yourself what boundaries you can set to protect the time you devote to those priorities. Start slowly. Building and protecting your boundaries is like building a habit. In *Atomic Habits* [26] by James Clear, we're taught that breaking bad behaviors in exchange for creating good habits begins with small, incremental, everyday routines that compound into massive positive change. He teaches us to focus on getting one percent better every day. Don't go cold turkey into full priority and boundary mode. Focus on one small boundary you can master first, then add on the next one.

Your priorities and boundaries shouldn't be a secret. Don't be afraid to share your priorities with people and the context behind the choices you make. Share the priorities that are relevant for them to know, based on your relationship. An explanation can help them better respect your priorities and boundaries. It can also turn them into supporters of your journey.

My cancer treatment took a huge toll on my body. When it was all said and done, I was out of shape and squishier than I had ever been. My priorities shifted, again, to regaining my physical fitness. The more I shared with people that priority, the more supportive they were.

Don't let fear of judgement get in the way of you being open and honest about the life you are trying to create for yourself. This is a life where you have the ability to advocate for your priorities, by setting clear boundaries.

You Can't Do It All

Remember those women I referenced in the beginning of this chapter? The ones who seem to have it all together? These women have learned an important fundamental truth. You *can* have it all, you just can't have it all *at the same time*.

They have mastered the art of prioritizing the things that are more important to them and giving most of their time and attention to those things. They set clear boundaries and fiercely protect them like they're the most precious resource they have. But the truth is that they are dropping balls all over the place. However, those mistakes barely register to them because they aren't what's most important.

This is why most women have a visceral reaction to any conversation about work-life balance. Deep down, we know that it's all a lie. There is absolutely no way for us to balance all the things we need to do with all the things that other people need from us. Nevertheless, we still search for some sort of balance in our lives. We feel like utter failures when we can't seem to find it.

I want you to imagine a tightrope walker standing on a wire suspended between two buildings, ten stories in the air. In her hands is a long pole. As she takes each careful step, the pole is in constant motion, adjusting weight or attention where it is needed. We are the tightrope walker. We may be able to find balance in tiny snippets of time, but as we continue to move forward, we're required to adjust where we put our attention, constantly.

There's only so much room on that pole, too. Overloading ourselves with other people's priorities or things that don't matter would be like carrying extra people on our shoulders and other stuff on the pole. It makes achieving balance nearly impossible. Inevitably, we'll drop things or fall off the wire altogether. We can only carry so much. Let me say that again, **you cannot do it all**. You can only carry so much.

The women who are more likely to succeed learn this critical lesson of self-advocacy. Get really good at doing the things that are most important to you. Say no to the things that you don't have time for, don't matter to you, or you can't succeed at. Be intentional, selective, and focused. The most successful women I know don't take on more just to prove they can handle a lot. The most successful women are good at identifying their priorities, setting boundaries to protect them, and saying no when it doesn't serve their goals.

That doesn't mean that they avoid risk or run at the first mention of failure. There is an important differentiation between saying no to things that don't matter or that you can't succeed at and saying no to things that scare you.

It took about twenty months for me to complete all of my treatments for breast cancer and be cleared for unrestricted physical activity. During that time, my once active body was sedentary, restricted, and too tired for the activity I once lived for. Once I was cleared to begin working out again, I couldn't wait to get back to it. The one glaring problem was that my body didn't feel the same. It didn't move the same. My once strong muscles were weak, my limber body brittle and unmoving. It was defeating. Cancer had already taken so much from me and it seemed at every corner it was taking something else, something I loved.

I committed to start working out again and to start slow. I started two days a week with a trainer and focused only on strength training. I went to a facility that had members mostly of retirement age, primarily so I wouldn't feel bad about how weak I truly was. "Certainly," I thought, "I am stronger than them." After about six months there, I decided it was time to upgrade to a group fitness gym. I chose one that had one-hour classes throughout the day and combined cardio with strength training. It took me months of saying I was going to join to actually make the move to do it. The only roadblock was my own fear.

I possess a fear of failure and perfectionism (I'm so lucky). I'm basically afraid of doing things that I can't do perfectly the first time. What an asinine philosophy! I have to constantly work to override the little voice in my head that tells me I will look like a fool, that people are judging me, and that people will know that I don't know what I'm doing.

When I joined the group fitness gym, I had to constantly override that voice that says, "You're not in shape enough," or, "People are looking at how slow you're going on the treadmill." It takes a lot to do the things that scare me. It takes a lot to worry less about looking dumb or out of shape or slow or weak and focus more on the work. Some days I can't even override the scenarios in my head enough to even show up to class. I let the fear take over so much that I can't even talk myself into going.

There's a fine line between the things that you can't be successful at and the things that scare you. So many of us live in our comfort zones. It's cozy in there, that's why it's called your *comfort zone*.

Our comfort zone doesn't require us to do new things, try stuff that's scary, or get uncomfortable in any way. In our comfort zone, we stay the same. We do the same things, we hang with the same people, we take the same kind of jobs at the same kind of companies, we make the same mistakes, and we lean into the stuff we're best at. It's safe that way.

You cannot ascend in leadership or in your career in your comfort zone. There is no growth in your comfort zone. If you want to grow, if you want to ascend, you have to get uncomfortable. There is no growth in your comfort zone and there is no comfort in your growth zone. We must get better at recognizing the line between knowing this doesn't serve us and we can't be successful at it versus knowing it scares us and we're afraid to fail.

Doing the things that scare us is where we experience growth. We must learn to override our natural instincts and socialization as women to play it safe. We must be willing to take risks, try new things, do it imperfectly, and fail, because if we don't, we won't ever *grow*. If it doesn't challenge you, it doesn't change you.

I didn't say yes to my group workout classes because I knew I could succeed at them. In fact, I was pretty sure I would fail. I said yes because they were important to me. I was (and still am to this day) wildly uncomfortable most of the time, failing miserably, and wondering if people are noticing how slow I'm actually going on the treadmill. But I've gotten better at overriding that little voice that tries to scare me away from the growth opportunity.

We have to be careful with saying no. It's a powerful tool and it can be wielded for both good and evil. Too often we say no from a place of fear, for self-preservation, or self-protection. Those limiting beliefs get in the way of growth. We feel like we are making an empowered decision, like we're self-advocating and we're proud of ourselves. In reality we're not. We're running away from something that scares us. Be careful with the word no. Use it intentionally.

Chapter 10:

What Do You Want From Your Career?

Shattering your own glass ceiling requires you to know what you want from your career. It's not often an easy question to answer. After all, many of our careers will take a very winding path. What you want today in your career could look dramatically different than what you wanted five years ago and what you will want five years from now. It's somewhat dangerous and confining to be married to a particular path or a particular destination.

I've talked to marketing executives turned ministers, chemists who are now patent attorneys, and healthcare executives turned tech visionaries. We shouldn't be rigid in our vision for our own futures. We can't predict what opportunities will present themselves along our career paths or how we'll feel about our careers when they do.

What we can determine, at any point in our journey, is what our passions are. We can also determine what work, environments, and experiences give us joy. We can identify what skills we desire, what types of supervisors or bosses we want to work for (if any), and what types of companies are a match. You may not know the titles of the next three jobs you'll have or the next three companies you might work for, but you can better define what types of experiences you'd like to have and the types of companies you'd like to work for. Chances are, after your next step, you'll need to redefine your desires because they will likely evolve as your career does.

Begin by identifying what career values are important to you. What are the things you want in a work setting, job, or organization? Is being recognized for your achievements important? Maybe your ability to earn a great income or benefits matters. Do you need to be in an environment that allows you to be creative, autonomous, or secure? Do you want growth opportunities and a clear path into leadership? Do you want a certain level of power organizationally to make decisions or lead others?

Understanding what those things are for you and which are most important is a critical part of self-advocacy. Below is a partial list of career values to begin from. Take a moment to identify what your must-haves are in your career right now. Then identify a few of what you would like to have.

Certainly, we would like to have most of the below list, but it's unlikely that we will find the perfect job, employer, and boss, all with the perfect compensation package, rolled into one (yet a girl can dream). You need to decide what you are willing to concede on and what is non-negotiable.

Choose from the below list (or define some of your own) to identify a handful of career must-haves and a few like-to-haves. Put them in rank order and keep them somewhere safe (like in your Success Journal).

- Be recognized for your achievements
- Work with enjoyable colleagues, doing work that is fun
- Do work that helps people
- A workplace that inspires and encourages creativity and innovation
- The ability to earn a good living/great total compensation
- Opportunities to learn, be challenged, and grow
- A work space that is physically and emotionally comforting
- An opportunity to learn a new skill or work in a new industry
- Autonomy or independence in your work
- Work that requires rational or intelligent thought
- A job that affords time away to enjoy leisure activities
- A location close to where you live
- A job that allows freedom to hold your specific beliefs
- Work that gives you a level of power, control, or authority
- Positive feedback or public credit for your work
- A job, company, or workplace that provides security in pay or employment
- A job or workplace that gives you prestige or respect from others
- Diverse responsibilities or work functions
- Opportunities to travel for work
- A sense of belonging
- A culture of inclusion and respect
- Opportunities for advancement
- A great manager/supervisor
- Competent leadership, staff, and team members
- An industry with opportunities for growth

- Desired company size
- Positive corporate image and corporate integrity
- Opportunities for a flexible schedule, work from home, or target hours

Early in my career, I wanted opportunities for travel, a clear path for personal and professional growth, upward mobility opportunities, and to do work that was fun. As my career and life evolved, the location of where I worked mattered more and the opportunities to travel mattered less. Upward mobility became a bigger priority for me, too. Once we had children, everything turned on its head. Suddenly a flexible schedule, more security, and less travel were important. Yet, the desire to not lose any power was important, too. Our career values change and evolve.

You learn lessons about what you need and want from each job, company, and boss you work for. You learn that your supervisors and their management style might matter more than you originally thought. You might learn you like working for a smaller business, instead of a large corporation. Maybe you realize that free snacks and an amazing coffee bar in the office are the perks you need. Each of these lessons are important to remember and listen to as you continue to ascend in your career.

The shifting priorities don't require us to find a new job. These shifts can give us guidance on what we should be asking for or working toward in our current roles. It gives us more clarity on where we should be advocating for ourselves at work.

Too often, we march into our annual performance evaluations without a clear vision of what we want or what to ask for. We ask for more money, more vacation, or more professional development dollars. We could be asking for so much more and we don't even realize it simply because we haven't taken the time to think it through.

Chapter 11:

What Do You Want From Your Relationships?

In my household, laundry is a task that I gladly take full responsibility for. I am particular about how things are washed and folded, what is line-dried versus put in the dryer, and I am careful to inspect my children's clothing for stains. Most importantly, I can fold a fitted sheet. Each Saturday, everyone brings their hampers down to the laundry room and I set off on my routine to sort, turn right-side-out, stain treat, wash, dry, and fold our family of four's laundry. The clothes are returned to the hampers and that is where my duty as the laundress stops. Everyone is required to carry their own hampers (the kids with some help) back up to their rooms to put away their own clothes. Everyone except my husband, apparently.

Week after week my husband's hamper sits in the laundry room overflowing with clean clothes, neatly folded and sorted by type. Each morning he showers and then makes the trek downstairs to rifle through his hamper of clean clothes and get dressed.

If you're sitting there aghast, you have a sense of my perpetual pain as my husband's hamper, full of clean clothes, transforms into a rummage sale bin. Sure, I could make him do his own laundry. I could dump them on his side of his bed until they're folded and put away. I could carry the hamper upstairs and put it away myself. All of those things could be effective, but what I want is for my husband to put his clothes away in a timely manner each week and to stop using our laundry room as some sort of makeshift satellite closet.

Week after week, the hamper remains a permanent fixture in what I once called my Zen space. I took great pains to renovate our laundry room to my exact specifications so that I would enjoy the space and find solitude and peace while in it. Yet day after day, I walk into the laundry room and rage at the sight of my husband's laundry basket, right where I left it. I altogether lose my cool when my husband then commandeers *my* hamper for his dirty clothes since his hamper is still down in the laundry room.

He then ends up with two hampers full of clean clothes while my clothes sit in a precarious stack on the laundry room counter, where they could topple to the floor or into the sink at any moment, thus requiring refolding. At that point, I totally lose my cool on my husband. I somehow manage to string enough words together for him to understand that my rage is a result of his laundry hamper(s) and he swiftly takes off for the laundry room while accusing me of "coming in hot". The rage subsides for a couple of days until we quite literally rinse and repeat.

I don't tell you this story to lambast my husband. Our marriage is actually quite balanced and healthy. I would be lying though if I didn't tell you that it has taken a lot of work, introspection, self-awareness, and self-advocacy on both sides to get our relationship there. It's not perfect either, *clearly*. I tell you this story to illustrate an important point: if you're struggling to identify what you want in your career, you probably don't know what you really want in your relationships either. Instead, you silently endure things in your relationships because you don't have a clear picture of what you really want or how to effectively articulate it.

If you lack self-awareness related to your skills, strengths, growth opportunities, and weaknesses in your career, you're probably lacking self-awareness related to your skills, strengths, and weaknesses in your relationships, too.

I know what my strengths are in my marriage, but I also know what my weaknesses are. However, I'm not just talking about *romantic* relationships. Our friendships and familial relationships leave a lot to be desired. Frankly, I know a lot of people (myself included) who still have a lot of work to do to self-advocate in their relationships. I've lost a lot of friendships over my life and when I look back, I often try to figure out where the friendship went wrong.

Regardless of what's on the surface, the relationship often dissolves because we couldn't be (or didn't want to be) the person we needed each other to be. What we wanted and needed from each other became too incongruent and the relationship fizzled.

Sure, there are lots of surface-level manifestations of that underlying reason: they didn't spend enough time with you, they didn't give enough support, they didn't show an interest in your life, they only called when they needed something, etc. No matter what reason you give on the surface, what it boils down to is you weren't the people you each needed. You couldn't or wouldn't give them what they needed or wanted from the relationship.

I need my husband to take his laundry upstairs every week and put it away. Am I going to end my marriage over it? No, but I am responsible for self-advocating for what I need. Too often we sacrifice our own needs and desires for others. We silently suffer while contorting ourselves to give the other person everything they need and to be the person they want us to be. For months (maybe even years), I would walk into the laundry room and experience immediate rage at the sight of my husband's laundry still sitting there. Yet, I wouldn't say anything. I would just be mad *in silence*.

As women, we're really good at being mad in silence. We've been conditioned to bury our anger because society labels it as unattractive or crazy. So, we develop the mantra of "keep the peace" and bury the anger, never asking for what we want or need.

Yet, I'm convinced that many of us would have trouble articulating what we want or need from a partner, friend, or family member if we were asked. We've been so conditioned to ignore those feelings and we've gotten so good at burying them that they're difficult to access.

The work of self-advocacy is to understand who we are and what we want, first. That isn't just who we are and what we want in our careers, but in all facets of our lives, particularly in our relationships. When we understand ourselves, we are able to better recognize the things that are incongruent or not serving us. That doesn't mean it's not difficult to come to these realizations. Letting go of friendships or relationships that once meant a whole lot to you shouldn't be taken lightly.

I realized years ago that I am the crisis friend. I'm the person you call in a personal or professional crisis. I will pick up the phone, drop everything, jump in a car or airplane, and be there when stuff hits the fan. I'll clear a spot on my calendar to grab a coffee to listen. I'm cool and calm in the chaos. I'm strategic as we move through it and problem-solve. As a result, I tend to be the person my friends (and some of my family) call when there's chaos.

These same people also know that I do not have space for shooting the breeze. I'm not going to call you just to catch up. I follow you on social media. I like the pictures of your kids and your pets. I send you memes and reels late at night while I lay in bed drifting off to sleep. I love you and you know that I am always there, but I'm not the ever-present, know-what-you-had-for-lunch friend.

There are relationships in my life that needed me to be something different. They wanted something different from me than I could give. As a result, those relationships fizzled away. It's not that I didn't value those relationships or didn't want to try to be the person they needed. I did try. It just required me to stretch myself too much and I couldn't sustain it.

While losing those relationships was painful, constantly trying to be someone you're not is more difficult. Those relationships take a toll on us. They empty our buckets, so to speak. I don't think I had the right words to define why this happens in relationships until recently. I always just saw those relationships as draining, but I kept pushing through them because the people mattered to me. There are many of us who are that way because we are so relational by nature.

We tell each other that we can't pour from an empty bucket as a way to encourage self-care. What we really need is better self-advocacy. We need to be more in tune with what we need in our relationships, what other people are asking us to be, and where those things are completely incongruent. Then we need to get good at asking for what we want and setting boundaries in those relationships to protect them.

Just like I told you earlier, you can't do it all and you can't have it all (at the same time). You can have the things you really want when you prioritize and set boundaries. Similarly, you can't be everything to everyone. You can have positive and rich relationships with people *with* priorities and boundaries. When we lack priorities and boundaries in our relationships, they become problematic or toxic.

What Do You Want

What do you want from life, relationships, and your career? If you can't immediately answer that question, it's time to get clarity. Self-advocacy requires us to be able to articulate what we want. We find ourselves stressed, burnt out, overwhelmed, and unhappy because we haven't advocated for the things we need and want. Establish what your priorities are in life, relationships, and careers. Set boundaries to protect them. Get good at saying no to the things that you don't have space for. Understand that you can't do everything and you can't be good at everything. What you can do is be really good and really focused on the stuff that matters most. The rest is just a bonus.

Part IV:

How To Ask For It

Chapter 12:
Mindset Matters

As women, we have been taught that we can't just *ask* for the things we want. We've been conditioned to believe that if we do ask for what we want, we're going to be told no, then shamed or belittled for even asking.

We're suppressed into the good girl role that teaches us to keep quiet, not cause a fuss, not be any trouble, and not complain. We tell ourselves that we're unqualified, undeserving, or unreasonable for the things that we want. We tell ourselves that it's not a big deal. We watch as our male peers are promoted, paid, and elevated more than us—time and time again.

The fear of asking for what we want is real. While shame and retaliation do happen, it doesn't mean we should stop asking. We must understand the possible consequences and outcomes of every ask. Prepare to pivot each time the answer is no.

I can't count the number of times I've been told no. They certainly outweigh the number of times I've heard yes. But **you don't get things you don't ask for**. The only way to get what we want is to take the risk and ask, in spite of what the answer might be.

Learning how to self-advocate can't be limited to knowing who we are and what we want. The most critical part is learning how to ask for the things we want. Asking for the things that we want requires us to master communication and leverage relationships. I don't want to oversimplify though. These topics could each be their own book and they can take an entire career to master. However, the only way we master them is through preparation, trial and error, failure, learning from our mistakes, and trying again.

I have bungled communication millions of times. While I didn't keep count of how many times I failed, I know it's only through that failure that I have grown in asking for the things I want, saying things in a way that people can hear them, and getting what I need more often than I don't.

As I said, we're never going to be perfect and we're not going to be great at it from the beginning. Mastery is earned through deliberate practice: focusing in on the areas where you need improvement, development, and growth.

Mastery requires us to do the work regularly and repeatedly. Don't give up because you hear no on your first try (or your ninetieth try). Don't give up because it feels awkward or uncomfortable either. That discomfort is growth. If it doesn't challenge you, it doesn't change you. That failure and discomfort are you on your way to mastering the skills you need to advocate for yourself in all areas of your life.

Negativity And Gratitude

Have you ever lain awake at night replaying the moment you yelled at your kids during dinner? Maybe you quasi-blacked out while driving, thinking about something you said at a work meeting and how stupid you probably sounded.

Perhaps you drifted off during a video conference meeting and were met with unwelcome feelings about something you said five years ago that you're still embarrassed about. Do you recall every negative thing every boss has ever said to you in a performance review? Yeah, me too.

Research has shown that the memories of negative events or experiences last longer than positive ones and they often carry more emotional weight. This trait is an evolutionary mechanism used to teach humans to recognize and avoid dangerous situations. As a result, negative outcomes are easier for us to remember. That's why we can only seem to remember the tiny bit of negative feedback we're given and forget most of the positive feedback included with it. It's also why we tend to outweigh the potential negative consequences and under-value potential positive outcomes. It's why we're afraid to advocate for ourselves. The potential negatives weigh heavier than the potential positives. That's negativity bias.

So, what do we do about it? Well, for starters, recognizing that negativity bias exists is an important step. If we understand that our brains will naturally weigh the negative more heavily than the positive, we can work to rebalance those instincts. Here are a couple of ways to override the negativity bias that is impacting your ability to self-advocate:

- Listen carefully when receiving feedback and make notes of what is being said. Be intentional in recording both constructive criticisms and positive feedback. Too often we merely record what we have to work on and not what we're told we are already doing well. Be intentional about recording both. Try making two columns in the place you're taking notes, one for positives and one for negatives.

- When attempting to make a decision, many of us naturally make a pro-con list. Even if there is an equal number of pros and cons on the list, our brains will put more emotional weight on the cons. Instead of creating an equal list of pros and cons, aim to add five additional positives to your pro list before you make a decision.
- Don't talk to your best friend that way (that's you). Negative self-talk can be significant for us as women. I catch myself doing it all the time. "You're such an idiot Jessica," I'll say in my head (and sometimes stuff that's much worse). Recognize that negative self-talk and do a check-in with yourself. Ask yourself those "what" questions we talked about. What is making me feel this way? What can I do differently next time?

It's easy to get sucked into a spiral of negativity and focus only on the bad stuff that is happening to you. When you feel yourself stuck in a negative place, focus on shifting your mindset to gratitude. What are the things in your life that are good? What's going well? Chances are there are good things and bad things happening in your life simultaneously.

Negativity bias won't go away. It's intrinsically a part of who we are. Recognize it and work to override the tendency to weigh the bad more than the good.

When I was diagnosed with breast cancer at the age of thirty-nine, I could have easily been sucked into the negativity spiral of asking, "Why me?" Instead, I was determined not to let my cancer diagnosis or the long road of treatment define me. I didn't want to look back on that time in my life and have it marked as the year I had cancer. I started a gratitude practice the day I was diagnosed.

We live under the false assumption that our lives are like a single railroad track. On that track is either good stuff or bad stuff happening in our lives. But our lives are much more complex and robust than that. We can experience challenges and joy or bad and good at the same time. Yet, because our brains are naturally wired to place more significance on the negative, it's easy for the good in our lives to get drastically overshadowed. This is why spending time focused on the positive is so important. It helps us to see that even in the midst of challenges and adversity, we can experience joy and positivity.

However, there is an important differentiation between seeing the positives in our lives (gratitude) and toxic positivity. People often assume the two are synonymous when they are actually different. A gratitude practice asks us to acknowledge that while there is adversity in our lives, there are always things to be grateful for.

I can have cancer and be going through a difficult treatment protocol while also being grateful for:

- Great doctors
- A world-class cancer center twenty minutes from home
- Great health insurance
- A job that allows me to balance treatment and work

- Supportive family and friends helping me navigate the journey

I get to experience all the emotions, not just one side of them. It would have been easy to have a pity party about my diagnosis. Frankly, no one would have blamed me either. I could have also ignored all the negative emotions and only saw the bright side. Free boob job, am I right? Gratitude acknowledges the complexity of human emotions and also names them.

Toxic positivity, on the other hand, asks us to only look at the positives of a situation and ignore any of the negatives we face. It asks us to take any negative emotions and put them into a locked safe, never to be opened again. That's not healthy or realistic.

I wanted to be more balanced during my cancer journey. My gratitude practice provided me with a healthy way to stay out of the spiral of negativity that I have fallen victim to before. I would get up every morning and sit with my cup of coffee and my journal. I would write the things I was grateful for, the things I needed help with, the things I was scared about, and the good that was happening in my life. Sometimes I would write for five minutes and sometimes I would stop myself at five pages.

The result? I had minimal side effects during my cancer treatment. Every hurdle I encountered never felt like a big deal. Without gratitude journaling I could have launched into a spiral of defeat, making recovery harder by amplifying the little things into a much bigger deal. But I didn't. I focused on the positive amidst the difficulties and it made all the difference.

I won't sugarcoat this: asking for what you want is hard. Working up the courage to speak your mind, and ask for the things you need or want from life, relationships, or work, is scary. What if the answer is, no? Truth be told, the answer is no *a lot*. Understanding how to bounce back from those no's is critical to our success as women.

During my conversations with successful female leaders, I would always ask them, "What is the one skill or trait you think is critical to a woman's success?" Overwhelmingly, their answer was resilience.

Our ability to bounce back from adversity and failure, as well as persist in the midst of it, is essential to our success. Understanding the role that negative thoughts and gratitude can play in our overall mindset is important. Keeping a positive and grateful mindset helps us to bounce back from the inevitable rejection we will face when we choose self-advocacy.

Chapter 13: Communication

I have spent much of my professional career teaching people how to effectively communicate and build relationships. I can't even tell you how many books there are on the topic, likely too many to count. Communication is a tricky topic because it does not exist in a vacuum. Culture, societal expectations, gender, race, physical appearance, and accent (and much, much more) play a role in how communication is perceived, interpreted, and rejected or accepted.

The major challenge with effective communication is understanding the difference between the intent and its impact. Just because we intend for someone to hear our words and the meaning behind them in a certain way, does not mean they will receive those words in the way we intend them. Herein lies the problem with communication. We have limited control over the way our words are perceived by any person or group.

That lack of control is amplified by the fact that we are female. It should come as no surprise that women are held to a different standard in communication. The expectations are different for us compared to our male counterparts. We are evaluated more frequently on our communication, while men are more often evaluated on job performance [27]. When people are asked what characteristics they look for or desire in a leader, they often cite assertiveness, honesty, confidence, and decisiveness. These are traits that are seen positively when demonstrated by men in leadership. Yet, when women demonstrate these same traits, they are perceived negatively [28].

Women are expected to be kind, collaborative, and nurturing. However, these traits don't always demonstrate the conventional expectations of individuals ascending to higher levels of leadership. People want us to be assertive, honest, direct, confident, and decisive. Yet, when we are those things, we're labeled difficult, angry, and irrational. We're ultimately penalized for exemplifying the traits that are expected in leaders.

The same double standard applies in communication, too. In practically every annual review I've ever had, I was penalized for my communication, and only my communication. In every other measurement of performance, I was knocking it out of the park. I was exceeding expectations in every other category. Yet, time and again, I was told I was too honest, too blunt, too assertive, too intimidating. My supervisors would tell me that I could be nicer, I could say things with a smile, I could soften my directness a bit. Every time I received that feedback I was confused, wondering why any of it was a bad thing. I didn't understand how my communication was a problem. The alternatives to my direct communication style seemed more problematic. Yet, supervisor after supervisor gave me the same feedback.

On occasion, I would push back. I would ask why being honest and opinionated was a problem. I would express my confusion at the notion that assertiveness and decisiveness were negative traits. Ultimately, I believe the feedback about my communication inevitably stalled my ascension into leadership and my ability to be seen as someone who could lead others.

So, over time and through lots of failure, I slowly started to adapt my communication. I started to learn the finesse of delivering information in a way that other people could hear it and receive it. If you didn't just roll your eyes at that sentence, I'll roll my eyes for you. It sounds like I'm suggesting that women communicate in the way men want us to communicate. It sounds like I'm suggesting that we tiptoe around delicate egos, placate those in power, and play a game to get ahead. That is not what I am suggesting at all.

I found that learning the finesse of communication is like playing a game where no one tells you the rules. The only way you learn them is by watching and listening to the other players. The first rule you have to learn is what matters to the other players. On the surface, it can appear that everyone wants the same things and that the goals are shared. Underneath, everyone has their own priorities. Understanding what matters to people allows you to tailor your communication so they can hear it as aligned with their personal goals.

For a number of years, I've been working with an organization on launching an initiative focused on building a more inclusive and equitable workplace culture. The organization's culture is already great, but they continually strive to be greater. As the initiative was preparing to launch, part of my role was to meet with all the stakeholders to help get buy-in. There is a pretty clear business case for diversity, equity, and inclusion initiatives in business and the conventional wisdom on the topic is pretty substantiated [29].

However, I knew I couldn't roll into each conversation and data dump on each team. I had to figure out what mattered to them, what they were specifically dealing with, why they might care about the initiative, and how it might improve their corner of the business. Once I understood what mattered to them, I could get their buy-in by sharing information, data, and case studies in a language they could understand. This helped them understand how the initiative connected to what mattered to them as leaders and stakeholders.

We often make the mistake of communicating to people from our point of view or experience instead of *theirs*. As a result, the message doesn't always translate properly. It's like putting on someone else's glasses. The prescription is all wrong and we can't see quite clearly. Instead, we have to communicate through the perspective, experiences, and priorities of others.

This work requires us to be really good at listening, asking lots of questions, and diligently setting our own opinions and beliefs aside, all in an effort to understand someone else's. Speaking less, particularly as a woman in male-dominated environments, can open us up to patronizing comments, mansplaining, and people misjudging our skills. Listening, much like everything else we do, requires us to delicately balance competing priorities: establishing ourselves as competent and valuable while also ensuring we listen enough to learn what matters to the others in the room.

Being a great listener requires two things: having a genuine interest in others and asking good questions.

We ask a lot of bad questions. How are you? How's your family? How was your vacation? What's wrong? These types of questions are called short-answer questions. They illicit a one word to one sentence response. The responses are short because the questions are very specific in nature. Because they are looking for very specific pieces of information, they get short, specific responses. We didn't ask someone to tell us every detail about their family vacation. Many times, we don't even care. We're just being friendly, and we want the other person to have the perception we care. So, we get used to asking really bad questions.

Being a good listener requires us to ask better questions. Better questions give the person we're listening to permission to expand on their answer. This requires us to ask open-ended questions. Open-ended questions start with phrases like:

- Tell me about
- I'm curious
- Talk to me about
- Help me understand
- Explain to me
- I wonder
- Describe to me

These phrases elicit longer responses and allow you to listen to what the other person chooses to share. When given permission to talk at length, individuals are often surprised by their own responses. The conversations are more interesting and less mundane. This allows you to show a more genuine interest in the person you're talking to, what they're saying, what they care about, and what is important to them.

As we listen to their responses, avoid the urge to interject and one-up the individual who is speaking. We have a natural tendency to want to make connections with others. Often, we will find whatever connection we can, no matter how meaningless it might be. The result is that we interrupt the person we're talking to and make the conversation about us. The person we're talking to never gets to finish what they were saying.

Listening more and interrupting less allows you to better tailor your communication to the other person's needs or goals. That helps ensure that both the intent and the impact of your communication are aligned.

Let's imagine you schedule a meeting with your supervisor to ask for more responsibility at work. You sit down, prepared with your list of accomplishments, and launch into an epic monologue covering why you want the promotion, why you deserve it, and how you've worked hard to earn it.

While everything you shared is true, the reasons are about you, not your boss. Your boss doesn't disagree with what you're saying. Instead, they make a handful of excuses to either stall you or blame someone else for their inability to give you a promotion. What if they just didn't feel like going to bat for you? What if the risk of advocating for you wasn't worth the reward? What if your request wasn't connected enough to their goals instead of yours and so the message didn't land?

Let's consider a different way. How could you communicate differently for that promotion by focusing on what matters to your boss, too? In that scenario, you would start by asking your boss what their priorities and goals are. You would ask about what things they want to take off their plate or delegate down. You might learn about their goals for the team or things that they would like to be spending time on but can never seem to find the time for.

You could then cite the work you've done and how you have contributed to the team's outcomes. You could mention things that your boss is overwhelmed with and how you could take those tasks off their plate, freeing them up to do things that are more important. You might bring up the working relationship you have with clients that would allow a seamless handoff of certain responsibilities to you. Those examples speak directly to what matters to your boss. Now, your boss might feel more willing to advocate for your promotion because they can see the direct benefits to them, as well.

This is the toggle of communication I'm talking about. I'm not suggesting we should pander to delicate egos or adjust our assertiveness so others aren't uncomfortable. I'm suggesting we learn how to match intent and impact by advocating in a way that people can understand—in a way that motivates them as much as it motivates you.

But what do we do with delicate egos? What about the people who disagree with you? What about the people who will never take you seriously, see your communication for what it is, or treat you fairly?

That's where the second rule of communication comes in: relationships matter. When we have established relationships with people, our communication is more accurately perceived, we make fewer assumptions, disagreements are easier to resolve, and we're able to know where our self-advocacy will be most effective. Without relationships, a lot more of our communication is ineffective.

I make these recommendations about communication based on my experience as a white straight cisgender woman. It would be irresponsible not to acknowledge the additional and more significant challenges that women, with identities that intersect with womanhood [30], face. BIPOC (black indigenous people of color) women and black women, in particular, face greater scrutiny for their communication. They are overwhelmingly perceived as more angry, assertive, and hostile in their communications [31]. Most of this is an unfair compounding of bias related to their gender and race.

This is why relationships are so interconnected with communication. When people know us, they read our assertiveness as passion, not anger. They interpret our blunt communication as honesty. They label our decisiveness as leadership and not merely being bossy. They're less likely to interpret directness from a black female as anger. They're more likely to take our words at face value, instead of creating false perceptions of what's happening. At minimum relationships empower people to confirm that the impact matches the intent of the communication and avoid misinterpretations.

Is it fair that we have to be so intentional about our communication when many of our male peers don't? Obviously not. It's frustrating that women must methodically build relationships so we can self-advocate effectively. It's not fair we have to play a game to get ahead, but unfortunately, we do. We can't mindlessly float through our careers. We have to move intentionally and thoughtfully. Our communication and our relationships have a major impact on our ability to ask for the things we want.

All of this goes back to my point at the beginning of the book: *this is an inside job*. We have to actively fight the forces oppressing us while simultaneously participating in them. It's the only way we shatter our glass ceilings, ascend into leadership, and become valued voices at decision-making tables. Part of that inside job requires us to build relationships and be highly connected *inside.*

Chapter 14:
Relationships

Every summer my family takes a trip to the Outer Banks of North Carolina. Every year since my daughter was born, we rent a house on the beach with a couple of long-time friends and their crew of children. For a week, we toggle from swimsuits to pajamas and then back to swimsuits. The early mornings are spent sitting on the deck, coffee in hand, staring at the Atlantic, talking about everything from family drama and jobs to sports and politics. The evenings are filled with laughs and antics that could fill an encyclopedia full of inside jokes.

When you share this type of proximity with other families year after year, the relationships are deep, intimate, and meaningful. We've seen each other through hard times, shared amazing memories, and witnessed each other at our worst.

One year, as we huddled around the long dining table finishing up dinner, one of the husbands said, "Jess was the only friend of Lauren's that I was intimidated by."

I remember meeting Brian. I was in town speaking at a conference near where my best friend from college, Lauren, lived. She and I met up for dinner and a few drinks. She wanted me to meet this guy she had been dating. Brian showed up about forty-five minutes after us in a leather jacket, carrying his motorcycle helmet. His presence was imposing. He was tall, dark, and built like a linebacker. His personality was kind, warm, and funny. I liked him immediately. More importantly, I liked him for my best friend.

I remember Lauren sharing with me, prior to his arrival at the restaurant, that I was the final approval. All her other friends loved him, and they loved them together. For the life of me, I can't recall grilling him or treating him icily during our first meeting. Yet, there he stood in the beach house more than seven years later admitting to being intimidated by me. Obviously, he's not intimidated by me now that he knows me, but he *was.* Why?

Unfortunately, I've found this to be the case in many of the relationships of my life. People meet me, then eventually get to know me and become a friend. Later, they fess up to the fact that I intimidated them before they knew me. Sometimes they're even willing to admit that they thought I was mean. I used to be surprised by the comments, but now I've come to expect them. I've begun to learn that it's the price I pay for being an assertive female who advocates for herself, is willing to call things out, and says the things that most people will only whisper about to their closest friends.

When I became CEO for the first time, I put a wall up between myself and other people, particularly my employees. I was intentionally guarded because I thought that was what a leader was supposed to be. I thought that the more about myself that I let my employees know, the less they would respect me. I thought I had to be perfect, so I hid the imperfect parts of myself as a leader, mom, and person.

In *The Five Dysfunctions of a Team*, Patrick Lencioni [32] shares that trust is fundamental to high-functioning teams. Trust, before all else, must be built in order for teams to be effective and high-performing. I know from my years of teaching communication and relationship building that there is only one way to build trust with others: through vulnerability.

People get wildly uncomfortable when I share that being open about who you are with others is the key to trust and is necessary to relationships. There is no other way. Yet there is some sort of societal conditioning we go through that tells us that vulnerability is a sign of weakness and should be avoided at all costs.

We have to challenge our assumptions about what being vulnerable really means, particularly at work, in our careers, and as leaders. I see a lot of leaders afraid to admit when they've made a mistake, missed a deadline, made a bad hire, or acted irrationally. I see a lot of leaders pushing their teams with unrealistic expectations of performance while they fail to contribute to the collective work. I see a lot of leaders, managers, supervisors, and bosses with a general lack of empathy for the human beings who work for them. These situations demonstrate a clear lack of vulnerability in leadership. It's a lack of trust. It's a lack of relationship.

Conversation is a regular part of the human experience, especially at work. Many of us spend the majority of our workday in conversations. Having a conversation with someone means you made a decision to engage with them. Whether out of necessity or desire, that decision lands you in a conversation. Those conversations can be as meaningless as the one I have every day with the crossing guard at my daughter's school (we discuss the current and predicted weather for the day) or as meaningful as the ones I have with my girlfriends (we discuss the stressors of being a mom and working at the same time).

What differentiates a conversation about the weather and one about the stress of motherhood marks another decision—a decision to *care* about the conversation you are having or the person you are having it with [33].

Too often, we have meaningless conversations that have little to no impact on us or others. They leave our memory as quickly as we leave the conversation. When we decide to care about the conversation or the person we are having it with, the conversations are more meaningful. When I see bad leaders or bad behavior from leaders, I see a lack of empathy and compassion. I see a lack of *care*. We haven't invested in the people we work with. We haven't invested in the conversations with them. Even when we care, we're still just having conversations. We don't yet have relationships. We still lack trust.

To build relationships and trust, we have to decide to show people who we really are, to open up, and to be vulnerable. That's super scary.

Every day, we wake up and put on our armor. While we don't literally put on chain mail and pick up a helmet and sword on our way to work, *figuratively we do*. The armor hides all our imperfections, mistakes, history, trauma, and insecurities. It protects us from being hurt, judged, and the real us from being seen. It shields us from vulnerability. The truth is that we're all just a bunch of broken, imperfect people walking around hiding from one another.

You can't build a relationship (and trust) with someone until you're vulnerable, until you take some of that armor off. Does this mean we need to strip all the armor off until we're naked, sharing our deepest, darkest secrets with the people we work with? Goodness no. Perhaps we start with a single piece of armor and bit by bit, show people more of who we are. All relationships are built over time by sharing pieces of ourselves with others. This requires us to be more open and real with people at work and as leaders.

The only way to get someone to share pieces of themselves with you is to share pieces of yourself, first. As a leader, it's our job. As we climb each of our own career ladders, vulnerability becomes imperative to our success. The relationships we build along our career journey become critical to our ascension and our success as women.

Just like my best friend's husband, when people know us and have relationships with us, they have more accurate perceptions of who we are. Similarly, our communication isn't misinterpreted or misconstrued as often because they know who we are as a person.

In theory, this all makes sense. But so many of us still struggle with the actual act of vulnerability, especially at work. There is always this perceived line that we shouldn't cross of getting too personal at work.

There are certainly things about ourselves that don't have a place in the work environment and there are definitely things that are better kept private. So how can we be vulnerable, at work? Here are a few suggestions:

- Talk about the lessons you've learned from failure. While it might seem counterintuitive to talk about places where you have failed in your career or in your life, talking about failure can be an easy way to be vulnerable. Sharing failures makes you more human. Reframing the failure to talk about the lessons you've learned allows you to not only be vulnerable but also demonstrate resilience and a growth mindset. Don't be afraid to talk about times when you've failed and what you learned.

- Admit when you're wrong. Sometimes admitting when you made a mistake is the hardest thing to do. Being willing to admit when you're wrong is a way to be vulnerable while also demonstrating humility and building trust. It helps others to feel safe admitting when they're wrong and builds an atmosphere that demonstrates that everyone is valued.
- Highlight other people's strengths, openly. Drawing attention to the skills of other people on your team is a way to build trust. It's like indirectly saying, "This person is better at this than me and I am openly admitting it." That's disguised vulnerability. Sometimes it's the best kind because it makes others feel good in the process.
- Talk about your life outside of work. Share pieces of who you are outside of work. My team meets every Monday morning. We spend the first fifteen minutes talking about something fun we did the weekend before and sharing pictures of dogs, kids, family, vacations, etc. It's not dramatically vulnerable, but that little window into each other's world is an important way to build trust and relationships with each other.
- Avoid the difficult, personal stuff. Deep personal trauma or drama that is occurring in your life shouldn't be dumped on other people at work. The question to always ask yourself is, "Am I sharing this so people can trust me and my

> work? Or am I sharing this because it will make me feel better or to garner sympathy?" When I was going through cancer treatment, I was very intentional about sharing my treatment plan and what was happening with my team, but not for pity or sympathy. I wanted them to know when they could expect me to be in and out of pocket for work-related stuff. I avoided the ugly, hard, and personal stuff of my journey and saved that for my relationships that were more personal, outside of work. Too much vulnerability can be a burden for people. Use it wisely.

While vulnerability seems counterintuitive, it's necessary for our success. Pretending to be perfect and have it all together is a shield that we hide behind to avoid showing who we truly are. It makes people trust you *less.* But vulnerability builds relationships. Vulnerability builds trust. Trust builds a better understanding of who you are and how you communicate. It allows you, as a woman, to be more accurately seen. It allows you to self-advocate more effectively. When we have healthy relationships, our communication is more accurately perceived, and our self-advocacy is more successful.

Take a moment to think about the relationships you have at work. Are there relationships that you could invest in or strengthen? Are there people that you don't have relationships with, but should? Are there relationships that could benefit you now or even down the road? Make a list of some target individuals to strengthen or build relationships with. Use that list to intentionally connect to help advance your career.

Ask For Help

Learning how to ask for help is an important part of self-advocacy. Finding people to support your journey, advocate for you in areas that you can't, challenge you, encourage you, and inspire you are critical as you ascend toward your glass ceiling. It is vital to find allies to support you in your life and in your career.

That seems like a no-brainer, but I don't think we as women are particularly good at it, especially when we exist in male-dominated environments. We assume that those around us will see all the work that we do and know what we want and need. Then, if we deserve it, they will magically bestow us with the things we want—even though we haven't communicated what we want to anyone.

This is the crux of the issue. We often don't know what we want or need and can't effectively ask for it from the people who can or want to help.

I once participated in a professional mentoring program for a little over a year. It matched seasoned, professional women with young professionals for a period of three months. There was an impression that we were matched using the robust assessments we took about our talents, but I can't really confirm that was true.

My first mentee wasn't able to articulate what she wanted. At our first monthly meeting I asked her what I could do to support her and her response was, "I just want to learn from you." Cool. "What exactly do you want to learn?" I responded. I spent the remainder of our first meeting sharing with her my personal and professional experience and asking her a series of yes-no questions to figure out how I could help her. I ultimately helped her update her resume. It felt like a waste of time.

A later mentee had a much clearer picture of what her goals were, but she didn't really know what she wanted help with. We ultimately landed on a few ways I could support her, but I ended up serving in more of a coaching role than a mentor role. After about a year of bad matches, I gave up on the program. It was a drain on my time, and I didn't feel like I was helping in a way that leveraged my talents.

I think we've got the idea of mentorship all wrong. The way that mentorship programs are set up in many environments makes the assumption that a single person can be all things, to all people, all the time. We cannot expect to shove two strangers together for a set amount of time with the simple instruction, "Help each other." It doesn't work. There's no relationship and there's no trust.

We cannot expect trust, particularly the level of trust that is necessary to share your personal career desires, aspirations, and struggles, to manifest from thin air.

As women, we need a lot of mentors and we need them all at the same time. They need to be people we trust, have relationships with, and have supported us in certain ways in the past. What we really need is a *board of advisors*. I'm not the first person to suggest that professionals have a personal board of advisors. This isn't a new concept and I'm not poo-pooing mentoring programs, either.

I am suggesting that internal (and external) mentoring programs should have different goals. These programs should focus on helping women connect in meaningful ways to build trust with others as a means to build their own personal board of advisors. Your board of advisors should target individuals in three categories:

First, people we admire. They may be individuals who are a few steps ahead of us on a career path that we desire for ourselves.

They might be a leader that is a few layers above us in our organization, too. They're likely in the same profession or industry as you. Perhaps they have a job you hope you have one day. They might even be people whose advice has been helpful in the past. These are the people you go to when you need direction, advice about the next steps, and help networking. They're generally people who can give you perspective on the industry and as a result, can be leveraged as you navigate your career.

Second, people who challenge us. These are people who ask lots of questions when you come to them for advice, but they rarely tell you what to do. They push you and offer a unique perspective, different from your own. They're honest and tell you what you need to hear. They don't placate you. You might feel confused or frustrated when you leave conversations with them, but that frustration often turns into greater clarity later. These are people who are great when you need someone to poke holes in an idea or a decision. They're great to leverage when you're surrounded by people who only tell you what you want to hear.

Finally, people who encourage you. These are the people who pump you with fluff and sunshine. They fill you with words of affirmation and serve as really great cheerleaders throughout your career. They're good listeners and they help you process the pros and cons of any situation. These are the people you can lean on when your confidence is low or when you're confronted with imposter syndrome. They're the people who will nominate you for awards and encourage you to chase opportunities you may not feel qualified for.

Each of these categories should have multiple people in them. You'll leverage the people at different times throughout your career. They might be former bosses, colleagues, or peers. They might be friends. You get to decide. It's your board! There is only one rule about who is on your board of advisors.

The rule is that you must be intentional about cultivating and maintaining relationships with these people over time. If you're not actively reaching out, checking in, and connecting, the efficacy of their role dilutes and they'll slip off your advisory board. It's okay if that choice is intentional, but if there are people whose advice is valuable to you, you must make plans to periodically (at the least) check in with them.

I had a supervisor in graduate school named Jeremiah. Jeremiah is someone who challenges me. In graduate school, I would often leave his office on the verge of tears. This wasn't because he was a mean boss but because he wouldn't just tell me what to do. I would leave so frustrated and angry. I'd stomp back to my cubicle in the grad office, have a little cry, maybe a good scream, and then I would sit there and fester, thinking about his words. I would replay the conversation over and over again.

Eventually, I would come to a decision and march back into his office, plop down in the chair across from his desk, and share my new plan, while he grinned ear to ear. His plan had worked. I had arrived at an answer through my own self-discovery.

Jeremiah is now the person that I call when I need to be challenged, when I need someone to poke holes in a plan, ask difficult and thought-provoking questions, or give me a perspective that I don't have. I never have to question whether he's telling me exactly what he's thinking. I know he never sugarcoats it.

Jeremiah is just one person I would consider on my board of advisors and he isn't a female. He doesn't work in my industry, and I'm guessing if you asked him what I really do for a living he wouldn't entirely know. That's okay (I'm not always clear about what I do for a living either).

A board of advisors is a group of people that you trust, that you intentionally cultivate and maintain relationships with, and that you know you can rely on for advice, support, challenge, inspiration, or encouragement.

They help you know how to advocate for yourself better. They make the ascension toward your own glass ceiling less lonely and much more thoughtful. You don't need to march around your company, formally asking people to be your mentor. Leverage the relationships you have and focus on building new relationships. Then use those relationships for advice, insight, inspiration, and challenge, as needed throughout your career.

Chapter 15:
Allies

I believe there are a lot of well-intentioned men out there who believe in equality. They want to help women succeed at work and in their careers. However, they have no idea of all the ways that they benefit from a system that was built by men for the benefit of men. They're generally clueless to the subtle nuance and microaggressions that we, as women, experience in our everyday lives. They want to be allies, they just don't know how.

To be honest, there aren't great resources for men to learn how to be allies. The media often suggests men should take women to lunch and hire more women to their teams.

That is not being an ally.

If we want men to be allies for women we need to take responsibility for showing them how. We cannot expect them to figure it out for themselves. Teaching men how to be better allies is self-advocacy.

It's telling men, "Hey. I need help. Can you do this *specifically*?"

Imagine you have a standing weekly meeting with another team in your company that you and your boss attend together. One of the men in the meeting regularly ignores your comments or interrupts you when you are talking. Your frustration gets to a boiling point, and you lash out at him in the meeting.

You heatedly say, "I was speaking. Please stop interrupting me." Now you're labeled difficult and rude. You look emotional and unprofessional to the others in the room.

Let's rewind. Instead of lashing out at Loud Guy, you pop into your boss's office right after the meeting. You say to him, "Do you notice that Loud Guy ignores my comments? He usually interrupts me when I'm speaking, too."

Your boss is flabbergasted. He didn't notice.

You then say to your boss, "Would you just watch for it next week in the meeting? If you catch him doing it, would you say something to him or call it out? I don't want to do it and be seen as unprofessional." Your boss agrees and is now successfully engaged as an ally with a clear definition of how he can support you.

In the meeting the following week, Loud Guy interrupts you. When it happens, your boss makes direct eye contact with you, looking shocked that he missed it before.

Your boss then says, "Sorry, Loud Guy. I want to make sure you heard and acknowledged what Jessica just said. It was important." Loud Guy is noticeably jarred but turns to acknowledge your comment.

A few minutes later, Loud Guy interrupts you mid-sentence.

Your boss interjects, "I want Jessica to finish her thought before you share yours. Jessica, would you finish what you were saying?"

Over time, Loud Guy's behavior eventually wanes enough for you to feel respected in the meetings and when it does get out of hand, you can count on your boss to speak up.

That's what an ally might look like at work. The problem is that we often make the unfair assumption that men notice bad behavior and ignore it or choose not to take action. I prefer to begin with the assumption that they don't notice or don't realize it's problematic. Our job as women is to engage them as allies, to help draw their attention to the problematic behavior, and then ask them for help.

For the allies reading this book, here are some additional recommendations of ways that you can take action to be a better ally. While this is not an all-encompassing list, it is certainly a way to get started.

- Intentionally seek out women to listen and hear their stories of harassment, bias, and mistreatment in the workplace, and *believe them*. It's common for men to be totally oblivious to the injustices women, particularly BIPOC women, face. We often hear male leaders say, "We don't have a problem with harassment or bias. We have no reports of it." The truth is the data tells a different story. It's happening, it's just going unreported by most women because of fear of retaliation. A great step would be to start trying to understand the experiences of women at work and believing them when they tell you.
- In meetings that you have control over, ensure that female (and historically marginalized) voices are equitably represented and given equal voice. It's easy to call a meeting and

invite the usual suspects. Ally-ship asks us to challenge the status quo and take a hard look at the people in the room. What voices are missing? We know that diverse teams are more creative and more successful. If you're calling the meeting, you get to decide how diverse the room is.

- In meetings where you are a participant, pay attention to the women in the room. Are they sharing? Are they being interrupted? Are their ideas given equal weight and consideration? If not, use your privilege to ensure those voices are heard, their ideas are considered, and credit is given.
- In hiring practices, don't settle for a pool of male candidates because your hiring managers said it was the best talent available. Require diverse candidates and more than one woman in the hiring pool. A recent analysis published in the *Harvard Business Review* discovered that when there is only one woman in the hiring pool, there is statistically no chance she will be hired [34]. When the pool increases to two women, she has a fifty-fifty shot. Push your recruiters to look harder for talented women and demand more diverse hiring pools.
- Ask women you supervise what their career goals are, and what roadblocks or hurdles they're currently facing, and then use your privilege to help remove them. Herminia Ibarra indicates in a *Harvard Business Review* article that too few women are being sponsored by male supervisors and leaders [35]. As a result, women aren't getting high-level assignments that are critical to advancement into senior leadership roles.

- Connect women to powerful men in your organization and your network through personal introductions, not just casual ones.
- Every time you have a negative reaction to something a woman says or how she says it, try asking yourself, "Would I react this way if it was a man?" Confronting our own personal bias is critical to allyship. If you're not sure if bias is at play, take the time to build a relationship with that woman or talk through your interaction with her to raise your own awareness.

Men aren't the only people who can be allies for women at work. We need female allies, too. However, this is where it gets complicated. When I interviewed successful female leaders, I often asked them who helped them along their leadership journey. At first glance, their responses were all over the map. But then I broke the responses down by age range. There is a distinct line where the responses changed.

When I asked women over fifty, many of them could not point to consistent or prominent individuals who supported, advocated, and were allies for them along the way. They would often share stories of how competitive it was for women at the top. There were very few spots for women as they ascended their career ladder. As a result, when they did finally obtain those coveted spots, they had to protect them like the commodity they were. There wasn't space for more women. Many of the women above them treated them poorly because they were seen as competition.

However, when I spoke to women under forty-five, I found the exact opposite. These women referenced a collection of women in their corners, supporting, cheering, and creating space for one another. There were almost too many women for them to mention each by name. I personally fall into this category. There are almost too many women to thank. It would be unfair to attempt to list them all, I would invariably miss someone.

This is the mixed bag of the career world for women today. We have women who act as roadblocks. They put up fences and are fiercely protective of their positions of authority. They live from a scarcity mindset that tells them that there's only room for one. They believe other women are a threat to their position. They behave in ways that do not advance or demonstrate the best in our gender.

Then there are women who understand that their role is to ascend into leadership while simultaneously creating space for more women. They believe in pulling women up the ladder with them. They represent the best in women. This mixed reality makes it very difficult for women to determine who is an ally and who is not.

The good news is that women seem to be getting better at it. There are fewer and fewer women who are protective of their singular space at the top. There are more and more women who understand that the more women who are in leadership, the more successful we all are.

Either way, we have to seek out female allies in the same way we need to seek male allies. We have to be intentional about communicating what we need help with and directly asking for it. They may not be able to advocate for us in the same ways as male allies will, but there will be ways that female allies can advocate for us where men cannot.

Communication and relationships are critical to self-advocacy. Asking others, particularly men, to help us advocate more effectively is essential to our success. When I ask women if they have allies, most often they offer up a few men who are supportive of women or supportive specifically of them and their careers. Yet, when I ask them to describe how they have been an ally for them at work, there are no clear examples.

This is the conundrum of allyship. We like the idea, but we're not particularly clear about how to be good at it. There's not a good manual for men and women in senior leadership positions on how to be an ally for women at work.

It's up to us to take a more active role in helping others learn how to be an ally for us, our lives, and our careers. We cannot expect others to know how to be allies if we don't help them learn where they can help us. We must advocate for others to be allies in the same way we advocate for anything else in our careers, lives, or relationships. Similarly, we must take responsibility for being allies for others in spaces where we have power. We not only have a responsibility to advocate for ourselves but also a responsibility to help other women up the ladder, too.

Do It Scared

I've struggled with fear, particularly fear of failure. Oftentimes, the fear is so debilitating that it will stop me from even trying. The fear is so strong I won't even ask. I won't go for it. I'm afraid of looking stupid, doing it wrong, getting rejected, or not being perfect. I'm a Type A, level five control freak. If I don't have all the details and can't control the outcome, I'm terrified. Having cancer helped me come face to face with my obsession for control and fear of failure. Since that time, I've been working with the mantra, *do it scared.*

"Do it scared" reminds me that fear should be expected. Failure should be accepted. Inaction is inexcusable. Failure isn't defined by doing it and not being perfect. Failure is defined as *never trying*. I let a lot of fear stand in my way in my life and career because I was afraid to fail.

When I left my first CEO job, I felt like a failure. In my mind, my plan for my future included all these amazing things at the company I was working for. When that dream and those goals were gone, I felt like I failed. From that point on, I let fear dictate every decision. It felt like my bold, ask for what I want, take risks, leap into the unknown personality disappeared as quickly as the vision for my future did. I confront my own fear of failure regularly by telling myself, "Be afraid and then do it anyway."

We don't get things we don't ask for. If you don't advocate for yourself, you won't ever get the things you want in your life, career, or relationships. Fear cannot be a barrier to self-advocacy. Do it scared. Ask for what you want and need in spite of fear of failure, rejection, not looking perfect, screwing it up, or whatever other reasons you're afraid.

Be afraid then do it anyway.

Ask

Let's get as practical as possible here. You've done the work throughout this book. You know who you are and what you want. We've talked about relationships, communication, mentors, allies, and fear. You're ready to advocate for yourself.

How do you do that? What are the practical, tangible, and actionable things you can do to advocate for the things you need and want in your life? I wish there was a single script for that. It's just not that easy. Every situation and relationship is so nuanced that it's impossible to give specific words to say.

What I can tell you is how to prepare. This way, you can set yourself up for success in having these conversations. Preparation is key. Here are the six things you need to do to prepare to advocate for yourself, especially at work.

1. Don't Hit Them Cold

Every time an employee schedules a meeting with me outside of their normal cadence, I immediately assume they're quitting or asking for a raise. Maybe it's irrational and maybe it's just me, but my muscle memory flinches every time I get this type of request.

In anticipation of said meeting, I begin analyzing literally everything that has happened between me and that employee in recent history. I work myself into a tizzy before the meeting even happens. My Type A control freak personality hates surprises. I know that most bosses hate surprises, too.

I like to know what I am meeting about before the meeting, even if it's bad news. I don't like getting hit cold with stuff face-to-face. I want to be able to react emotionally in private so that I can react professionally and logically in person. I want to have answers or solutions when I meet with people if I can. I hate giving non-answer answers like, "I'll have to get back to you on that." I don't like making promises that I can't keep.

Hitting me cold with big, important things doesn't allow me to be the best leader and help you to the fullest.

Don't hit people cold with the big things. This isn't middle school recess where you're breaking up with your first boyfriend and then running away. When you're preparing to advocate for yourself, give your boss an indication of what you want to talk about so they can come ready to have a productive conversation.

2. Use Data

When you're advocating for yourself make sure to come with data. Be ready to share the successes you've had and what those successes demonstrate about your skills, abilities, and potential. Share how you've contributed to the success of the business or your team and how you've met or exceeded the goals that were set for you.

In relationships and life situations, we have to come with data too. However, be careful in situations where data can be used as ammunition. Data doesn't work in personal relationships the same way it does at work. In personal relationships, it can make people feel defensive. Use your data when you're advocating for what you want in your career. Proceed with caution when using it with personal relationships.

3. Know Who You're Talking To

Obviously, I'm not being literal here. When you advocate for yourself, think through who you are talking to and how they will best receive the communication. How can you say what you need to say and ask for what you want in a way they can hear it? Do they need it on paper? Should you send an email before the conversation? Should you be face-to-face?

Also, prepare yourself for how they will react to your request and potentially what concerns, questions, or rebuttals they may have. Maintain a good handle on their goals. Understand what words might incite negative emotions and take the conversation to an unproductive place. Be sure you think through each individual you are talking to before advocating for yourself.

4. Build The Relationship Before You Need It

You should have a relationship with the individual before you self-advocate to them. Think through who the people are who can help you advance your career and get what you need in life and relationships. Build those relationships *before* you need them. Sometimes the mere idea of building a relationship with some-one so you can use them later on is troublesome for people. Let's reframe this understanding.

We're not using people. We understand the power of connec-tions and that relationships with others allow us to better advocate for the things we need. The relationships are primary, not second-ary. The support, help, advice, advocacy, ally-ship, and mentor-ship are merely a benefit of the relationship. You're merely giving yourself the opportunity to experience those benefits by seeking the relationship first.

5. Be Clear About What You Want

I once had an employee ask for a promotion. They had been with the company for a number of years but wanted to take on additional leadership and wanted a bigger title that represented that additional leadership. When I asked them what additional responsibilities they wanted, they couldn't tell me. When I inquired further about what title they wanted, they couldn't tell me.

There is nothing more frustrating than when people try to self-advocate but don't have clarity about what they want. It's like telling me you're hungry but not telling me what you want to eat.

When you get ready to self-advocate in relationships, in life, or in your career, make a list that clearly defines what you are asking for. Make it simple to understand. The clearer you are about what you are asking for the easier it is for leaders to say yes or negotiate where they can.

6. Prepare to Fail

What will you do when or if you fail? What happens when your self-advocacy doesn't work? Preparing for an alternative outcome helps you bounce back from failure quicker.

Part V:

When It Doesn't Work

Chapter 16:
This Won't Work

Perfection does not exist in the human experience. You won't get this right one hundred percent of the time, nor will advocating for yourself be effective every time you do it. Failure should be expected. The important question is, what are you going to do when you fail?

There have been times in my life and in my career when I advocated for myself and it didn't work. That failure left me standing at a crossroads. I had to choose to keep things as they were or change them.

Keeping things the way they were meant staying in a reality that I didn't want for myself. Changing my situation required making difficult decisions I didn't really want to make. This is the crux of the issue with self-advocacy. It often sticks you in the middle of two options where neither is the obvious or easy answer.

I had been advocating for less travel for several years with an employer. My travel calendar would temporarily get better after I would advocate and then things would go back to the way they were.

The demands of the job and the demands of our clients just required extensive travel. I could have delegated the work to someone else, but that also meant I would risk losing the clients (not to mention the commission). I was forced to choose between career and financial success or better personal balance. Having both was impossible. No matter how much I advocated for less travel, nothing could change the reality that my job required it. I was faced with two options: make less money and take a step back in my career to be home more or sacrifice my home life for professional and financial gain.

To some of you that might seem like an easy decision, but for me, it wasn't. Up to that point, my career was everything to me and the money was nothing to snuff at. But what I wanted was to be a mom who was present and active in my kids' lives. I didn't want to be a mom whose suitcase was perpetually unpacked and repacked. I didn't want to miss school field trips, dance recitals, and baseball games.

However, my job afforded our family a certain lifestyle that we had grown accustomed to. Giving it up and scaling back felt hard and scary. Ultimately, I left the job I loved, at the company I helped grow, doing work I was passionate about, with people who were like family to me. It was the hardest decision I have ever made.

I stood at a crossroads, juxtaposed between two decisions where neither of them was ideal. I didn't want to have to choose, but I did. Sometimes advocating for yourself requires you to make decisions you don't want to make. It requires you to change jobs, end relationships, confront others, set boundaries, disappoint people, and leave the ordinary for the unexpected.

Those actions are so counter to how we have been conditioned as women that they feel almost alien. From a young age, we've been raised to support, love, care for, and sacrifice ourselves for others. Making decisions for ourselves, for the benefit of ourselves, is a terrifying notion. Even for me. Even today.

I think this is why the self-care movement has become so popular in our current culture, particularly among women. We're beginning to push back on the expectation that we, as women, live our lives in complete service to others. We don't want to sacrifice ourselves completely. The self-care, treat-yo-self mentality is a tiny glimpse of true self-advocacy. Still, it's not enough.

Advocating for yourself shouldn't be a treat. It shouldn't be viewed as something that is special or outside what is normal. It should be commonplace and routine.

Every Mother's Day my husband diligently asks me what I would like to do to celebrate. Every Mother's Day I ask for breakfast in my pajamas at the dining room table and then to be left alone. I want to lay in my bed and binge an entire season of a show (any show) on Netflix. I don't want to be responsible for figuring out what to feed the tiny humans for lunch and answering their endless requests for snacks. I don't want to fold a piece of laundry or look at a messy room.

While the day feels like a delightful little escape, it also reminds me of all the places where I need to do a better job of advocating for myself at home. It reminds me that my partner is perfectly capable of handling all the responsibilities of our family. If I'm feeling burnt out or resentful for the amount that I'm doing, that's first and foremost *on me*.

Have I asked for help? Have I talked to my husband about better balance in the responsibilities of our home and family? Have I just assumed that he won't take on more when in reality, I've never asked?

It's not just the physical labor in our family either. It happens with the emotional and mental load we undertake, as women and as mothers, too.

Mental And Emotional Labor

There I was, standing at my sink brushing my teeth and washing my face, preparing for bed. My husband walks into the bathroom to brush his teeth.

As he loads his toothbrush with toothpaste and looks at me through the mirror, he says, "Emery needs to clean her room when she gets home from camp tomorrow. Have you looked under her bed?"

I wipe the freshly splashed water from my face and say, "Okay, but you'll have to handle that. I won't be home. I have class." Every Thursday for the last two years I've taught a class for emerging female leaders. It runs from 12 p.m. to 4 p.m. practically every Thursday. Every week my husband has to be reminded to get the kids from school or camp or wherever they may be. Generally, he's forgotten. Sometimes he's scheduled things during that time, which requires me to figure out a new pick-up alternative.

Since school was out, I knew that picking up our daughter from camp wouldn't register as a task he had to do. So, in an effort to curb the chaos, I sent him a calendar invite, four months ago, when I registered the kids for summer camps. I also put a special note on the weekly calendar that hangs on the door to the garage.

The calendar lists any relevant activities going on in the household and often indicates what my husband needs to handle.

This week, I put a special note on the calendar reminding him to get our daughter from camp on Thursday and specifically walked him to the calendar to point out that he needed to get her before the week began. Despite my efforts, here I stand in my bathroom while my husband spins into a frenzy of stress because he scheduled a pre-vacation haircut during camp pick-up. As he scrolls his phone determining that there are no other haircut appointments available before we leave for vacation the following day, he yells for our daughter.

As Emery walks into our bathroom, he begins to instruct her that she needs to be standing outside camp ready for him to pick her up at noon and no later. That stress-filled request sends our rule-following firstborn into a stress-induced meltdown.

"But Daddy, what if my teacher doesn't let me out in time? We're not allowed to leave unless our parents come in and get us. I can't be standing outside."

I escort our daughter out of our bathroom and back to her bedroom, calming her down by giving her instructions in the words she understands.

This is the emotional and mental labor that I haven't figured out how to completely self-advocate for. It's not just knowing my kids need stuff to do all summer and what things would be fun for them, but also knowing when and where to drop them off and pick them up, what to pack them for lunch, and what they need to wear or bring.

It's knowing how to say things in a way my kids will understand and what tone to use with each person in my home. It's knowing that my daughter has outgrown literally every pair of shorts she owns and now needs about four pairs of new shorts just for the summer. It's remembering that Oliver likes the crunchy Cheetos and not the puffy ones and that Emery likes the nacho cheese Doritos, not the cool ranch ones. It's knowing the names of their friends *and* their stuffed animals.

Listen, I have a great partner at home. Some of this imbalance is of my own making. I took on the load because I've been conditioned as a woman to do so, yet I haven't advocated for something different. When I have, my husband has happily picked up the slack. Frankly, I do it so I can control it.

I can be easy to blame other people. To blame our partners, friends, co-workers, bosses for the fact that we're stressed, overwhelmed, and burnt out. To some extent, they bear some responsibility. However, we have to recognize a hard truth: much of this is a product of our own making. Yes, the patriarchy and traditional gender roles are to blame. We don't have to accept it. We can advocate for something different. It's on us, just as much as it's on others.

When It Doesn't Actually Work

Here comes the hard part: There will be times when you advocate for yourself and it does not work. Maybe it gets better for a small window of time, then things go back to the way they were. Maybe you advocate, ask for something to change, and then they totally lose their cool. Maybe they look you straight in the eye and simply say no. What happens when your self-advocacy doesn't work?

The simple answer is, "I don't know."

I know that's not the answer you want to hear, but listen to me. I can't tell you what to do next. You have to decide. These situations aren't all the same. There's no formula or magic system to navigate when the self-advocacy doesn't work. There is so much nuance to these situations that it's difficult to apply a single set of solutions to every situation or relationship. This is where you have to pave the rest of the road yourself.

The decisions you make about what you will do when your self-advocacy doesn't work will be deeply personal and based on years of history, experience, and probably failure. You have to leverage all of those factors to determine what you do next. I don't know what the answer will be for you each and every time.

Here is what I do know: people don't change dramatically. Humans are capable of change. I know that is true. However, they don't change overnight. The arc of change is long and slow. If you are expecting a partner, colleague, boss, friend, or family member to change overnight you'll sadly wake up disappointed.

You have to ask yourself how long you are willing to wait for the changes to occur. At some point, you will either see a difference or you'll find yourself running up against the same challenges over and over again. At what point, do you make a change? How long are you willing to wait?

You are not for everyone. Oof. I learned this lesson the hard way through a lot of pain and disappointment. I struggled with being labeled as too much, too intense, and facing rejection for being myself. Not every relationship is a match. You're not going to mesh with every boss, supervisor, or colleague you meet. You will not fit in every corporate culture.

If you keep butting up against the same obstacles in the same place or with the same person, it may be time to face the fact that you are not for everyone. The person or place you keep having issues with may not be for you.

The ends (and beginnings) of things are always scary. Sometimes we're faced with a situation where we know that we have to end it, whether it's a relationship, a job, a volunteer opportunity, or a career. Ending things, particularly when you don't know what's next is really, *really* scary. Changing from something you know, no matter how bad, to something unknown, feels illogical.

I've said many times, "The devil you know is better than the devil you don't know." While that feels true, in lots of cases we never know what's waiting on the other side. It could be, and lots of times is, much *better*. We can't let the fear of an end or a new beginning deter us from making the decisions we need to make to advocate for ourselves and build the future we want.

It's better to fail than to stand still. *Failure means you've tried.* It means that you sought to do things differently or to try something new. Each of those failures takes courage. Each of those failures teaches us something about the world, ourselves, or other people. Those lessons are valuable.

Failing is much better than being so paralyzed by fear that you do nothing at all. Staying in a situation that doesn't work for you is a decision based in fear: fear of the unknown, fear of failure, fear of change. Every day, we all make decisions to stand still instead of fail. Self-advocacy requires us to choose failure over fear. It requires us to move instead of standing still.

Knowing these truths is important for determining what to do when your self-advocacy doesn't work. Those decisions aren't easy. They often make you feel stuck between two seemingly impossible decisions.

That is the work of self-advocacy, though. It's being courageous enough to ask for the things you want and need from your life, relationships, and career. It's being willing to face the decisions that come afterward.

Regret

I talk to so many women who are unhappy in a situation at work, at home, in a friendship, relationship, or in their family. When I ask them if they have asked for help, asked for change, or advocated for themselves, the answer is often, no. I'm not blaming them.

We've been conditioned not to complain, not to make a big fuss, and not to be a nag. We continually seek to meet the needs and desires of others, at the expense of our own. It doesn't just happen in marriages with kids either. It happens at work, in friendships, and in families, too. So instead of complaining or asking for what we need or want, we sit silently suffering, wishing for something different. Afraid to ask for a change.

Stop it. You *can* ask. You're not being selfish.

Getting help or asking for help is not a failure for you as a woman, mom, partner, friend, boss or coworker. Let all that go. Let all those expectations that have been put upon women for centuries disappear.

We don't get things we don't ask for. We have to ask. We have to advocate for ourselves. If we don't ask, we'll never know the answer. If you feel like your life is not your own, your relationships are sucking the life out of you, or your career is not what you imagined for yourself, then it may be time to advocate for yourself.

I know you're scared. I know you're afraid of change. I know you're thinking through all the things your advocacy might affect and how dramatically different your life might look as a result (both good and bad). I know you're weighing the bad stuff far heavier than it deserves, too. I know you're worried the answer will be no. I know that worry puts you at a crossroads of decisions that you don't want to make. I know those decisions, the advocacy, and change or the failure, are all so scary. But do you know what the scariest thing is?

Regret.

After I interviewed all of those successful female leaders, looked at all the data, and determined the competencies, I took a look at that list and asked myself, "What's missing?"

Certainly, I was allowed to add my own spin on this since I was a successful female leader in my own right. As I reflected on the list and the conversations, I started to realize that what stood out wasn't what they did say.

What stood out was what they *didn't say*. As these women, myself included, looked back on their careers, none of them had regrets.

In all the conversations I had over the lessons they learned and what it took to ascend into leadership and shatter their own glass ceilings, I never once heard any of them say, "I wish I would have . . ." In fact, many times they would look back on their mistakes and see them as unexpected gifts, not missteps to be regretted.

When you're diagnosed with cancer, you're faced with a lot of choices. With my breast cancer, I was offered a number of choices about my treatment. Chemotherapy was a no-brainer. It was my greatest chance of beating cancer so the answer to eight rounds of dense dose chemotherapy was an easy yes.

Following my chemotherapy, I had to choose my surgery options. The cancer was only affecting my right breast, but I ultimately decided to have a bilateral mastectomy, which is an amputation of both breasts. I said yes to removing my nipples, even though I didn't have to because there was an early cancer spot closely behind it. I then had the choice to do radiation or not. I said yes to twenty-five rounds of radiation, five weeks, five days a week. Even though those were the harder options.

When my surgery pathology came back indicating that I did not have a complete response to chemotherapy, I looked for a drug or treatment trial so I could get more treatment. I found a trial and underwent nine rounds of immunotherapy and six months of additional chemotherapy. Even though it was the harder option.

After my reconstruction was complete, my incision split open four weeks after surgery. I was given the option to try saving the implant or to remove it. I chose trying to save it, even though, again, it was the harder option. It ultimately saved my reconstruction.

I made all those choices, sometimes taking the harder road by extending my treatment when I didn't have to, because I didn't want regrets. I didn't want to look back years later wishing I had done more and said yes to more treatment, even when the doctors didn't think it was necessary. I look back at many critical moments in my life and I don't have regrets. I advocated for myself, and while the result of that advocacy was often a more challenging or difficult road, it was worth it.

Staying the same or taking the easier route would have left me with regret. The only regret I have is not advocating for myself sooner.

You don't have to advocate for yourself. That's the truth of all of this. You get to decide whether to speak up for yourself or not. You get to decide to live the life you imagined or be in the reality you're in.

If you want more, you have to advocate.

Advocate for you. You can't wait for someone else to do it for you. You can't expect people to know who you are and what you want. You, and only you, have to ask for it. That's the only way you will shatter your own glass ceiling.

Build a New Table

There are women who have advocated for themselves and have repeatedly been denied. They've tried and tried to navigate within the system that men have built, play their game, and get ahead, and it didn't work. They've changed companies, careers, marriages. They've lost friends, alienated colleagues, and burned some bridges.

No matter what they did, they just couldn't infiltrate the system. They were never going to be invited to the rooms where decisions were being made. They were never going to be a valued voice at the table.

So, they made their own table.

There are countless examples of where women got sick and tired of trying to get ahead in a game that was rigged. They stopped playing it. There is an element of that here that we should consider, too. None of these tactics, recommendations, advice, or data is absolute. There will be a moment when we have to consider the alternatives to participating in the system that already exists while simultaneously trying to unravel it.

We can build a new system. We can put so much external pressure on it, that it collapses from the outside. We can build a better system, so much so that the old way and the old system becomes obsolete.

At this point, you might be thinking that I've just contradicted the whole point of the book. Wasn't the point to participate in the system that is oppressing us and then dismantle it from the inside? Didn't I say that fighting it from the outside wouldn't work? Yes, I did.

I also said that the patriarchy is strong and powerful. It's an intricate web or a seventy-five-legged stool. There is no singular way to dismantle a system that robust. As much as I hope what I just poured onto the pages of this book will work for you, I'm not under any illusion that it will work for everyone. In fact, I'm certain some of you will try and eventually determine that it would be easier to just build a new system.

You should. I'll be rooting for you.

I wrote this book because I've hit these obstacles over and over again. I become tired of it, too. I knew that women had been successful. I wanted to know how they did it so I did the research. I found the lessons and I wrote this book. Is it an entirely new system? No. But it's certainly not another leadership or business book written by a white man named John [36].

I worried constantly that what I found was just a bunch of women who learned how to act like men to fit into their world. I toiled over the possibility that what I had written was nothing more than a guide on how to act like a guy at work.

The more I tested these concepts on myself and with other women, the more I realized the concern was insignificant. The more I talked to women about these strategies, the more I realized that I had stumbled on practical, tangible, and actionable advice for women to advance their own careers, climb the ladder to leadership, and shatter their own glass ceilings. I've never been more excited to share a secret in my whole life.

When I left my last CEO job, I felt lost. I felt like I had just lost everything that I had worked for in my career. I left a great job. I left an industry where I was a respected voice. I left most of my professional network and the work that I thought I would be doing for the rest of my life. Let me say it again: I was *so lost.* I had to do some really deep soul-searching to discover that in the absence of that job, I found what I was truly passionate about.

What I found was that I don't want women to have to run up against the same obstacles, feel the same frustration, and make the same mistakes I did. I want women to have the roadmap to succeed faster, climb higher, and shatter more glass. I believe that equality is necessary and equity is required to achieve it. I believe that the world will be a better place when there are more women in rooms where decisions are being made. I've never felt more sure of something in my whole life. I won't stop until women are represented at every decision-making table.

That will require us, as women, to advocate for ourselves even more. I've never been more convinced of a solution. Self-advocacy requires us to know who we are, what we want, and how to ask for it.

Knowing who we are requires us to build our own internal and external self-awareness. To work to understand our values, strengths, weaknesses, and growth opportunities. To reflect regularly and on the spot, as things happen. To ask *what* and not *why* because asking why leads us further away from the truth. *What* helps us understand how to:

- Improve
- Do things differently in the future for a better outcome
- Grow in our understanding of how others perceive us, and if we don't know, to just ask
- Believe what people tell us about how they see us
- Fight against the imposter in our head

Knowing what we want requires us to:

- Define what our priorities are in life
- Take the time to understand what big rocks we need to put in our jar first
- Set boundaries around those priorities
- Protect them like the precious commodity they are

The amount of time we have is finite. We have to fill our time with what matters most. We must share our priorities and boundaries are so others can support and respect our goals.

Knowing how to ask for it means we must:

- Prepare for failure and fight against negativity bias
- Learn to communicate with others so that your intent matches the impact of the message
- Communicate in a way that focuses on their goals as much as yours
- Build the relationship.
- Ask for help

Relationships are integral to advocacy. Find your board of advisors. Be explicit with your allies about how they can help you and what they can do to advocate for you in the workplace, in life, and in relationships.

Know that in the end, this might not work. Your advocacy might put you between two decisions where neither is desirable. Advocacy often requires us to confront bad relationships, bad environments, and unhealthy situations. Don't let fear of change, failure, or the unknown stop you from trying.

The only failure is quitting. The only failure is staying still.

In the end, have no regrets. If you take the steps to advocate for yourself and go after the things that you want in your life, your relationships, and your career, you will see every step as intentional, even if you fail.

Speak up for yourself. Ask for what you want. Advocate for yourself with the same fervor and enthusiasm that you do for the people you care about.

Climb that ladder, ascend into leadership, shatter that glass ceiling.

This is what it takes to shatter glass.

Good luck. I'll be rooting for you.

About The Author

Jess Gendron is a women's leadership expert and culture strategist. As President & CEO of The Center for Leadership Excellence, she helps women strengthen their leadership skills so they can shatter glass ceilings and actively advises businesses on how to create inclusive and equitable workplaces.

With over 15 years of experience working in leadership development and coaching, human resource consulting, business leadership, and higher education, Jess is a respected and sought-after speaker and thought leader for businesses, non-profits, women's organizations, campus communities, and inter/national fraternal organizations. More than anything, she is passionate about working with girls and women across every age group, every type of organization, and at every level. Her day job allows her to work with professional women and connect with business leaders across industries to understand the challenges of women. Yet, Jessica also remains passionate about working with young women and girls to build confidence, teach self-advocacy, and prepare them for what they will face in the "real world".

In February 2021, Jess was diagnosed with triple-negative breast cancer. She has openly shared her journey with cancer and her subsequent path developing her own gratitude practice. She's passionate about helping leaders shift their mindset to be more positive and resilient.

Jess was named to the Indianapolis Business Journal's Forty Under 40 in 2021. She is an award-winning instructional designer and in 2018 was honored for her contributions to the Fraternity and Sorority Community with the Jack L. Anson Award from the Association of Fraternity and Sorority Advisors.

Jess is a wife, a mom, a dog lover, and a boss. Her favorite place in the whole world is the outdoors. She received a B.A. from Eastern Illinois University and an M.S. in Education from Indiana University, Bloomington.

Learn more about Jess at jessgendron.com

Endnotes

1. There are many, many books that I would recommend to inspire and ignite your feminist spirit. A list of reading recommendations can be found at jessgendron.com/readinglist.
2. Huang, Jess, Krivkovich, Alexis, Starikova, Irina, Yee, Lareina and Danoschi, Delia. *Women in the Workplace 2019.* USA: McKinsey & Company, 2019. https://www.mckinsey.com/~/media/McKinsey/Featured%20Insights/Gender%20Equality/Women%20in%20the%20Workplace%202019/Women-in-the-workplace-2019.ashx
3. McKinsey & Company and LeanIn.org. *Women in the Workplace 2022.* USA: McKinsey & Company, 2022. https://www.mckinsey.com/~/media/mckinsey/featured%20insights/diversity%20and%20inclusion/women%20in%20the%20workplace%202022/women-in-the-workplace-2022.pdf
4. Sarah Blakely is the founder of Spanx, an American intimate apparel company. She started her company with a personal investment of $5000 in 2000. In 2021 the company was valued at $1.2 billion. Her success is often attributed to her persistence and tenacity.
5. Whitney Wolfe Herd founded Bumble, an online dating application that gives women control over matches (in heterosexual relationships) that launched in 2014. In 2021, Herd became

the world's youngest, female, self-made billionaire when she took Bumble public.

6. Public interviews of successful female leaders can be found at ladies-leading.com.
7. Eurich, Tasha. *Insight: Why we're clearly not as self-aware as we think, and how seeing ourselves clearly helps us succeed at work and in life.* New York: Crown Business, 2017.
8. Morgenroth, T., Ryan, M. K., & Fine, C. (2022). The Gendered Consequences of Risk-Taking at Work: Are Women Averse to Risk or to Poor Consequences? *Psychology of Women Quarterly, 46*(3), 257–277. https://doi.org/10.1177/03616843221084048
9. A quick Google search will produce a plethora of definitions of intuition. This definition is a combination of how a dictionary defines intuition, as well as what the existing body of research on intuition says.
10. The 19th Amendment of the Constitution of the United States of America prohibits the United States and its states from denying the right to vote to citizens of the United States on the basis of sex. It effectively gave women the right to vote. Its adoption was certified on August 26, 1920.
11. Title VII or the Civil Rights Act of 1964 was originally signed into law on July 2, 1964. It prohibits discrimination based on race, religion, color, or national origin in public places, schools, and employment, but only includes sex on the basis of employment. The omission of sex was later rectified by President Lyndon B. Johnson through Executive Order 11375 on October 13, 1967.
12. Title IX is a commonly used name for the federal civil rights law in the United States that was enacted as a part of the Education

Amendments of 1972. It prohibits sex-based discrimination in any school or other education program that receives funding from the federal government. Types of discrimination that are covered under this law include sexual harassment, failure to provide equal athletic opportunities, discrimination in STEM (science-technology-engineering-math) programs, and pregnancy discrimination, among others. It prompted a considerable increase in the number of female students participating in organized sports.

13. Shirley Anita St. Hill Chisholm was the first African American woman in Congress (1968) and the first woman and first African American to seek the nomination for president of the United States from one of the two major political parties (1972).
14. Kamala Devi Harris is the 49th Vice President of the United States of America inaugurated on January 20, 2021. She is the first female, first African American, and first Asian-American vice president.
15. Traister, Rebecca. 2018. *Good and Mad: The Revolutionary Power of Women's Anger.* New York, NY, Simon & Schuster.
16. Data from McKinsey & Company Women in the Workplace reports every year since 2019 indicate that women are getting promoted less frequently at every rung in the ladder. That mere fact is making women's ascension into upper leadership much slower than men's. Teaching women how to self-advocate will accelerate their upward trajectory.
17. Strengths Finder 2.0 is an assessment and personal development tool developed by Gallup Education that identifies an individual's top talents. The foundational premise is to not focus on your weaknesses or becoming more "well-rounded."

Instead one should focus on becoming better at what they are naturally great at. https://www.gallup.com/cliftonstrengths

18. Colvin, Geoffrey. 2008. *Talent Is Overrated: What Really Separated World-class Performers From Everybody Else.* New York: Portfolio.
19. Dunning, David (1 January 2011). "*Chapter Five – The Dunning–Kruger Effect: On Being Ignorant of One's Own Ignorance.*" Advances in Experimental Social Psychology. Vol. 44. Academic Press. pp. 247–296. doi:10.1016/B978-0-12-385522-0.00005-6. ISBN 9780123855220. Archived from the original on 29 May 2020. Retrieved 20 December 2021.
20. Sandberg, Sheryl. 2015. Lean In. London, England: W H Allen.
21. LinkedIn. "Gender Insights Report: How women find jobs differently." Accessed August 10, 2023. https://business.linkedin.com/content/dam/me/business/en-us/talent-solutions-lodestone/body/pdf/Gender-Insights-Report.pdf
22. Imposter syndrome is viewed as a phenomenon that is common among high-achieving women. The phrase was first coined in1978, in an article titled "The Impostor Phenomenon in High Achieving Women: Dynamics and Therapeutic Intervention" by Pauline R. Clance and Suzanne A. Imes
23. Kristen Hedges, "How Are You Perceived at Work? Here's an Exercise to Find Out," *Harvard Business Review,* December 19, 2017, https://hbr.org/2017/12/how-are-you-perceived-at-work-heres-an-exercise-to-find-out.
24. Player, Abigail, Randsley de Moura, Georgina, Leite, Ana C., Abrams, Dominic, and Tresh, Fatima (2019). Overlooked Leadership Potential: The Preference for Leadership Potential in Job Candidates Who Are Men vs. Women.

Frontiers in Psychology, 10, 755. https://doi.org/10.3389/fpsyg.2019.00755.

25. *Friends*. 2002. Season 8, Episode 14, "The One with the Secret Closet." Directed by Kevin S. Wright. Aired January 31, 2002 on NBC.
26. Clear, James. (2018). *Atomic Habits: an easy & proven way to build good habits & break bad ones.* Penguin: Avery.
27. Silverman, Rachel Emma, "Gender Bias at Work Turns Up in Feedback," *Wall Street Journal,* September 30, 2015, https://www.wsj.com/articles/gender-bias-at-work-turns-up-in-feedback-1443600759.
28. Pew Research Center, September 2018, "Women and Leadership 2018". https://www.pewresearch.org/social-trends/2018/09/20/women-and-leadership-2018/
29. "TheBusinessCaseforDiversity,EquityAndInclusion,"Forbes, May 11, 2023. https://www.forbes.com/sites/forbesbusinessdevelopmentcouncil/2023/05/11/the-business-case-for-diversity-equity-and-inclusion/?sh=449781c22838.
30. Intersectionality is a framework for understanding how a person's social identities can combine to create different modes of discrimination or privilege or overlapping systems of discrimination and disadvantage. Simply, when you identify as multiple marginalized identities, the discrimination and disadvantage often compound. Similarly, when you identify as having multiple privileged identities, the advantages or privileges also compound.
31. Motro, Daphne, Evans, Jonathan B., Ellis, Alexander P.J., and Benson III, Lehman, "The 'Angry Black Woman' Stereotype

at Work," *Harvard Business Review,* January 31, 2022, https://hbr.org/2022/01/the-angry-black-woman-stereotype-at-work.

32. Lencioni, Patrick M. 2002. *The Five Dysfunctions of a Team.* J-B Lencioni Series. London, England: Jossey-Bass.
33. This general concept is discussed in a book I co-authored about the power of building meaningful personal relationships to change the world. Mattson, Matthew G, Gendron Williams, Jessica, Orendi, Josh. *Social Excellence: We Dare You.* Carmel, IN: Self-published, Phired Up Productions, 2011.
34. Johnson, Stefanie & Hekman, David & Chan, Elsa. "If There's Only One Woman in Your Candidate Pool, There's Statistically No Chance She'll Be Hired," *Harvard Business Review,* April 26, 2016, https://hbr.org/2016/04/if-theres-only-one-woman-in-your-candidate-pool-theres-statistically-no-chance-shell-be-hired
35. Ibarra, Herminia. "A Lack of Sponsorship is Keeping Women from Advancing into Leadership," *Harvard Business Review,* August 19, 2019, https://hbr.org/2019/08/a-lack-of-sponsorship-is-keeping-women-from-advancing-into-leadership
36. In the year 2020, of the 200 bestselling business books, only seventeen were written by women. That was equal to the number of business bestsellers written by men named John/Jon. Further, 2023 was the first year that there were more female CEOs (forty-one) leading S&P 500 companies than men named John/Jon (twenty-three).

Printed in the USA
CPSIA information can be obtained
at www.ICGtesting.com
JSHW080100040224
56566JS00002B/26